Lady Lara Asprey

Lady Lara is the founder and owne
business The Sloane Arranger, the UK's only Introduction Club
catering uniquely to people who are a little bit sloaney. She has
personally matched numerous couples from high society in and
around the London area and become the go-to person within
her extensive social network for people looking for a serious
partner.

Website: www.ladylaraasprey.co.uk

The Very British Rules of Dating

How to find and keep your perfect gentleman
(and yes, he does exist!)

Lady Lara Asprey

It's a So Vain Book

Published in Great Britain in 2014 by:
SO VAIN BOOKS Ltd
75 London Road
Oxford OX3 9BB

www.sovainbooks.co.uk
Email: info@sovainbooks.co.uk

The moral rights of the authors have been asserted

A catalogue record from this book is available from
the British Library

ISBN: 978-1-910869-01-7

Printed and bound by CPI Group (UK) Ltd, Croydon, CR0 4YY

MIX
Paper from
responsible sources
FSC® C004959

For my family and friends for their infallible support, for every woman looking for love and the one man who helped me find it.

Contents

Introduction

Welcome to the world of British dating. So awkward, so emotionally inept and so anything but clear. Through my many years as a successful matchmaker, I've often found myself asking how the British manage to so readily procreate when their approach to 'wooing' is practically non-existent.

This book aims to give charming and elegant ladies a glimmer of understanding, a sense of reason and rationale into the mind of the British man – particularly focusing on how to find, keep and understand the eligible ones, whom to many seem to be becoming ever few and far between.

But how do you spot the quality, eligible sorts? Where do you meet them? How do you keep them interested? And how on earth are you meant to really understand what they mean by reading between the lines?

Through simple rules of dating etiquette, this book contains all the useful tools you'll ever need to identify when a British man is a gentleman (yes, they do exist), why they never come and chat you up (god forbid!) and what a classy and refined lady such as yourself Can do about it – without seeming desperate. It also provides you with tips on how to suss out what kind of personality you're dealing with so you can decide, based on your priorities, whether to take things further before getting too emotionally involved.

Learn the tips and tricks I coach my clients, and find answers to common complaints including:

* You wonder how all the other couples you know ever managed to get together
* You think chivalry is dead.
* You find men only do what could be considered 'flirting' when they have had a couple of drinks.
* Even then, their idea of 'flirting' is fairly odd and can often involve ignoring you or failing to recognise your existence.
* Nobody seems to meet anyone when out socialising as people tend to be introduced through friends or at work – and you have exhausted all your options there (not that they were aplenty to begin with).
* You look great, but nobody ever comes to chat you up. Therefore, you assume the men can't be that interested.
* You've tried online dating, but just spent hours filtering out the quality guys from the rubbish ones, only to meet a few and wonder who they ate or how long ago that photo was taken.
* When a chap starts to text you, you have no idea what his motives are and spend ages trying to decode his messages – often enlisting the help of your friends as key advisors, only to still not have the foggiest what they mean.
* You wonder why a guy can't just bloody well pick up the phone and call you.

* When you start seeing someone, neither of you know when you're officially together as it's a bit awkward to bring it up really.
* Your last boyfriend expected you to tell him he loved you before he would reciprocate.
* Your last boyfriend thought romance was a night in getting you to cook while he watched something on TV, probably sport-related.
* You don't know where all the good men are hiding.
* Your thoughts on 'good men': they are all married, gay or far too old/young for you.
* Your past relationships have just sort of 'happened', you can't remember whether there was any particular wooing involved.
* You have just generally decided to give up hope.

If any of this sounds familiar, welcome to the very British world of dating. This is a world unlike any other on this planet, a world where nobody really knows what anyone thinks, feels or expects. A world where there is little wooing, little emotion and a lot of misunderstanding. A world where you can't say the word 'date' without feeling embarrassed, where you can't tell the world you find someone attractive for fear of really being seen to go out on a limb.

Why is that you ask? Well, British men often expect women to show them they are interested first before they make any sort of move, so we tend to stay in what I call 'flirtation stalemate'.

Now don't get me wrong, I'm certainly not saying our British men are bad. In fact, they are known and loved across the globe for their lighting-speed wit, brilliant banter and good old British charm. The quality men are, on the whole, pretty loyal and sincere when they finally do express themselves, and they are incredibly self-sufficient in comparison to many other nations. A good British man makes a wonderful partner and a great friend, is a supporter and believer, is ambitious and is driven. It's just that they often need a bit of gentle encouragement and light prodding to make them come out of their shell romantically, so to speak.

You see, in my humble opinion, this is fundamentally a cultural thing and not a sexist one. The British – and apologies for sweeping generalisations, there are obviously exceptions here – but, on the whole, we as a nation really don't like to talk to each other very much. In fact, it's pretty much socially unacceptable anywhere other than a pub or bar to strike up conversation with a stranger, and even then only within a certain vicinity of the bar itself (never at tables) and only really after a couple of drinks. Conversations are infinitely more enthused by all involved should there be the comfort of an alcoholic beverage close by to hold onto for support.

Similarly, we board a train or use the tube, and we pretend to ignore each other, literally like nobody else exists in the world. The only time we wake from our state of blissful disregard is when there is some sort of delay on the tracks and only then do we suddenly start to look around, giving each other short glimpses of eye contact and knowing nods or tuts. A much argued reason for us all behaving in this manner actually stems from the Industrial Revolution, when commuting was still in its early days and the classes that ruled the country at that time often had to share carriages. A peer who had to share a carriage with a commoner could not be seen to strike up conversation,

and so firmly ingrained in our culture is this sense of being...
rather un-chatty.

You see, avoiding one another and failing to acknowledge
that the other party exists is not because we are rude per se,
but because we are reserved. If we don't talk to people we're not
encroaching on anyone's personal space and are avoiding the
need to make small talk, which, unfortunately, seems to make us
all feel terribly uncomfortable and exposed. Why make conversation with strangers when people will hear you, or you will have
to say things about yourself that you would rather not divulge?
It's SO much easier not to bother.

These rather British customs make things slightly awkward.
It's not only that we don't particularly want to chat to strangers,
we also don't have a standardised way of saying hello. Whilst
several of our European neighbours comfortably kiss new people
they meet on both cheeks, our previously standardised greeting
of 'how do you do' has pretty much disappeared. Handshaking
is only predominantly left to formal occasions, so this confusion
leaves us a bit unsure about
what to say, what to do with
our hands or whether to
kiss one cheek or two.

It's no surprise, therefore,
that the UK has the largest
amount of users of online
dating than any other
country in Europe. This
online world lets both men
and women save themselves
from the painful art of small

The proportion of couples
meeting each other via online
dating or meeting sites has
grown from less than one in
ten (9%) in 2003, to 17% in
2008, and to more than one
in four (27%) in 2013'
The Future of Dating
Summary Report, eHarmony,
Third City and The Future
Foundation 2013[1]

talk and potential rejection that just seems so much easier in their eyes. Like many things in Britain, we opt for things that are convenient and time saving - but so are the ready meals we seem to consume so much of as a nation, and how often do they really taste that good?

Whilst several Latin-rooted nations have seemingly mastered the art of seduction (and cooking things from scratch by that measure), they get rewarded by their peers for successful dalliances. To these nations, the more notches on the bedpost, the more the man. The more romantic and suave, the more they are perceived as a charmer and 'good with the ladies', and the more respect they inherently receive from their peers. And more importantly, the better these men feel about themselves when they achieve romantic success from their approaches to seduction. It's perceived as a rite of passage to approach girls and get turned down, and it is wholeheartedly believed to be a good way to thicken skin and toughen up.

The British man, on the other hand, is often not defined the same way. Being 'tough' is very often measured by how much a man can drink without falling over, and when a group of chaps go out there's often a lot of mockery and 'banter' involved with regard to approaching girls. If a man does approach a girl and fails, he most certainly will not hear the end of it from his peers for the foreseeable future, so instead decides he may as well just avoid trying, unless supported of course with substantial amounts of alcohol. In fact, I have never known a saying more wrongly associated with a nationality than 'Dutch Courage', especially considering how much the Brits revel in both saying and embodying it. The thought of 'chatting someone up' is cringe-worthy and awkward and it cannot possibly be polite to interrupt someone, surely?

So in amidst all this rather odd behaviour we, as women,

'I have never known a saying more wrongly associated with a nationality than 'Dutch Courage', especially considering how much the Brits revel in both saying and embodying it'

have to carefully weave our way through the minefield that is the British dating landscape. We might go out with our friends and hope to meet someone at a bar (which, as we know, is one of the only places where it's socially acceptable to chat). However, when we return home, we remove the makeup and comb the coiffed hair that took us so long to do several hours before, and we realise that not one man came to say hello. Not only that, but there weren't even any attractive men in the whole place. With a gentle sigh of despair, we fall asleep and assure ourselves they will turn up when we least expect them. They might be going to that party next weekend... Or perhaps there'll be a chance at that work function the following Thursday? They must be out there somewhere, maybe it's time to give online dating another go? Then we start thinking about the men we turned down and wondering whether we should have given them a second chance. This feeling only seems to worsen when we check our Facebook account to realise that really unattractive girl two years below you at school has just got married, or that friend who got divorced the same time as you is now on her second honeymoon.

Sounds familiar?

Well, I too have been there, and I was exactly like you are. Not too long ago, I would regularly frequent and explore some of London's hottest spots with my rather glamorous girlfriends, only to be amazed by the distinct lack of potential eligible candidates, and the incredible lack of 'real' opportunities to meet men.

However, I'm here to tell you the tricks I've picked up along the way through my experience as a matchmaker and will give you all the tips I can to keep the momentum of your dating relationship progressing exactly in the way in which you would like it to.

So let's begin our little adventure. We're going to cover what to look out for in an eligible chap these days, where to find one, and the best ways to get your dates working in your favour.

Background to British Dating

How did we get here?

Before we dive into the depths of where to find these charming chaps, let's do a quick recap on how we actually got here as a nation – from a dating and romantic perspective I mean. Why are we culturally this way? Why is it that both women and men are so reserved and that dating and romance are inherently tougher than in some other countries?

Now, I'm the first to say I'm no historian, but I do love a bit of context to help paint the picture and set the scene. I have always been truly fascinated and slightly baffled by the British rules and behaviours, and while matchmaking my clients, I found myself trying to work out more and more why we all behave in the way that we do.

Being English myself, growing up I have been able to observe some of our most virtuous customs, traditions and behaviours. I have grown up watching rather awkward public school boys and girls become powerful articulators and orators, and I have similarly seen hard working people rise to achieve wonderful things through sheer determination. I judge nothing, but observe everything and have been keen to get to the bottom of why we have inherited such truly British behaviour and how, as a developed and increasingly international country, our ability to 'romance' has, in a way, ceased to develop and evolve. Therefore, with that in mind, I wanted to look back a little bit and reacquaint myself with how romance used to be in this country... well at least for the upper echelons of society over a certain époque.

Around the middle of the 19th century, Britain was the richest and most powerful nation in the world. It was the first country to industrialise, and for this reason it had a head start over other nations at that time, and it had also successfully built up a huge overseas empire including Australia, South Africa and New Zealand. The nation started to generate a great deal of wealth, and certain customs and traditions became more defined, especially for the aristocracy and upper classes, who, at that time, really wanted to find ways to enjoy themselves. Led and influenced hugely by the movements of the Royal family – who would frequent London from April to July – what was known as the 'British Season' peaked during this time. It became customary for the elite to leave their large country houses and descend upon London for balls, dinner parties and charity events. Events such as regattas and race meetings began to spring up on the social calendars and became increasingly popular.

Whilst a great deal of this was about socialising and politics, it was also hugely important to give the aristocracy opportunities to meet and marry one another. These court presentations actually started way back in the 1780s, and by the middle of the nineteenth century they were a hugely established custom and an incredibly important opportunity for ladies to meet suitable men. Young women from upper-class families who reached a certain age were introduced to men via 'Debutante Balls' such as the Queen Charlotte's Ball, where they would be presented to royalty to mark the fact they were old enough to be launched into society.

The Queen Charlotte's Ball

The Queen Charlotte's ball started back in 1780 when King George III threw a ball for his wife Queen Charlotte for her Birthday in May, in an attempt to raise funds for the maternity hospital in her name.

Taking place over two or three days, around one to two hundred girls each day would queue up in their carriages outside St James's Palace or Buckingham Palace dressed like it was their wedding day. It was only after their official presentation or 'coming out ceremony', that the beginning of the social season each year officially began.

The main goal was for women to be engaged by the end of the season and a young woman was encouraged to date and flirt whilst maintaining her virginity. Chaps were known as 'Debs Delights' and those who were questionable with regards their intentions were labelled NSIT (Not Safe in Taxis), MTF (Must Touch Flesh) or VSINMBQ (Very Safe in Taxis Must Be Queer).

The Ball almost became as famous for its 'Debs' as it did for the eight-foot white cake. Queen Charlotte was said to have requested a huge Birthday cake as one of the highlights of the occasion which was the centrepiece of the ballroom. Debutantes would line up to curtsey towards the Queen and in doing so, the general direction of the cake. For two hundred years from that point forth, the cake became a symbol of the monarchy and debutantes would continue the ritual of curtsying towards it. Some people do argue that the giant cake was one of King George III's mad periods.

In today's money, attending all the events of the typical season and equipping oneself correctly with the expected attire would cost around £120,000.

It was a tightly controlled and hugely elitist affair. Mothers of young women who wanted to present their daughters at these balls would have to make an application to the Sovereign court and could only do so if they themselves had been presented. If the mother had died, then an aunt, grandmother or close friend could assume the role on her behalf, but with such strict codes of etiquette, the aristocracy basically created a really rigid set of rituals and codes to keep out the undesirables.

Young ladies were bred as socialites and the Season aimed to equip them with poise and social skills required for marriage. Typically, after their 'coming out ceremony' they would immediately start to receive social invitations and would be frequently called upon by gentlemen, which often meant a chap would turn up at her house and say hello or leave his card. It's pretty astounding to imagine today, but a lady could attend up to 50 balls, 60 parties, 30 dinners and 25 breakfasts all in one season. How exhausting! If she didn't marry within two or three seasons, she was considered a spinster and complete failure to society.

And we thought we had it tough finding love today...

However, with the growth of the country's wealth, more 'new money' began to appear on the social circuit and many non-aristocratic families wanted to buy their way into High Society. 'Society Matrons' began to appear, who would essentially sponsor anyone willing to pay for the privilege of being presented. Therefore, what was previously considered a very traditional occasion started to become perceived very differently, and the exclusive air of integrity around the whole affair began to dissipate.

The last debutante was presented in front of the Queen in 1958, and is now looked back upon with bizarre nostalgia. In my opinion however, these rituals have culturally instilled into us Brits a sense of courtship and flirtation that requires a certain amount of 'prim and properness' without showing any real signs of intimacy. The culture of romance in Britain therefore developed not through getting to know one another personally per se, but through the correct codes of conduct and behaviour. It was really of the upmost importance, and any deviation from such strictly 'proper' etiquette would have brought the names of those involved (and their families) into total disrepute.

The more we bit into the 20th century, the more outdated and peculiar these rituals began to appear. With the revolutionary swinging 60s and the introduction of the contraceptive pill, men and women became more equal, and

'We had to put a stop to it, every tart in London was getting in'
Princess Margaret

these rather archaic courting rituals began to disappear. Women became more empowered politically, financially and socially. They could vote, they could work, they could own property and they could fundamentally decide, on their own, when they would marry and when they would have children.

This left, and I suspect still continues to leave, the British man slightly perplexed as to his role exactly and that inherently makes dating even more tricky than it's ever been before.

The Modern British Gentleman

Does he exist?

With the phasing out of archaic courtship rituals, the modern British world is a far more relaxed place. Gone are prescribed rules that define your status as a lady

'It is a truth universally acknowledged that a single man in possession of a good fortune must be in want of a wife' Jane Austen

or gentleman per se and old blue-blooded money thankfully no longer has the same clout as it once did.

But with that welcomed change, the British gentlemen have become regarded as somewhat few and far between. They are often perceived by the Brits themselves as a bit of a cliché. You know, that mumbling-fumbling-floppy-haired-Saville-Row-wearing-Hugh Grant-or-Colin-Firth-type stereotype.

Well, I would certainly tend to agree with this as there is no cookie-cutter definition of a gentleman and no gentlemen factory where you can press a button and they all come out being just like they are in Richard Curtis' movies. They really do come in all shapes and sizes and are incredibly hard to define. In my opinion, however, there are certain telltale indicators that can help you work out whether any chap is good and decent: a quality sort.

Often the assumption is that a quality man is a wealthy man, but, in all honesty, money has absolutely nothing to do with it, and very often those with more money can be found to be ever so undesirable from a dating perspective. If they have made money in a short space of time and are keen to flash it, they are often excited by shiny new things and, therefore, they will change their girlfriends as readily as they change their socks. Not what you want.

Another assumption that is often made is that these 'quality sorts', or 'gentlemen', were bred in British public schools, and whilst many years ago that might have been perceived to have been the case, today it's by no means necessary in order to qualify. 'A gentleman' is a quality, not a person. It's a characteristic not the output of an institution. It's a state of mind, a way of living and a mindset, not a romantic gesture, a fad diet or a fashion trend.

That's because a true 'quality sort' is an intelligent, humble, interesting, self-deprecating, composed, successful, generous, funny and kind man who will be committed to a long-term relationship to give you, an ambitious and intelligent lady, the sort of relationship and companionship you truly deserve. In today's modern world

A gentleman' is a quality, not a person. It's a characteristic not the output of an institution. It's a state of mind, a way of living and a mind-set, not a romantic gesture, a fad diet or a fashion trend.

though, it's often very hard to tell if a chap is a quality sort from the first couple of times you meet him. The natural British reserve kicks in and we struggle to find out much about the other person until we have met them at least three or four times, preferably with some one-on-one time and not amongst friends.

So here are my personal favourite telltale indicators of a 'gentleman', a 'quality sort', 'a dapper chap', 'a keeper' or whichever term of endearment you gracefully wish to bestow upon them. Now, it's worth noting that no chap will ever embody all of the below, as that would mean there is such a thing as a perfect man, and quite frankly, if you are setting your sights on finding one, you will be searching forever. However, you might like to refer to this list should you meet a nice chap and be wondering whether you might be onto a potential winner. Even if he displays a few of these traits, then that's a terribly good start.

These are supported with absolutely no factual evidence, but they are based purely on my own observations and sense of humour, and are to be taken with a good pinch of (preferably British) salt.

First Impressions

Upon first glance, it's often incredibly difficult to tell much about a chap. Today's daily commutes have an abundance of men tending to dress predominantly like each other, and it can be hard to distinguish a quality sort from everyone else.

There are, however, some small signs you can tune yourself into noticing that might help you out.

Overall appearance:

* He does not stand out; often the more classy the chap, the more he tends to blend in. This is because a true gentleman is not a 'Flash Harry' but is more a 'humble henry' (note the use of capitalisation).
* He does not believe hair wax should make the hair appear wet, nor pasted to a section of his head, nor artfully crafted to resemble motion (hair should not go up, there is such a thing as gravity, and only age should fight it – hair should not).
* The sleeves. This is an interesting one but next time you're at an outdoor function such as the polo or tennis, look out for how far a man rolls up his sleeves on a warm day. If they are mid-way between his hand and his elbow, this is far more refined than right over his elbow like he's about to start some sort of heavy lifting.
* He wears a tailored suit, which fits like a glove and will not droop too far over his shoes.
* If he's not wearing a tailored suit, he's certainly conscious of how to buy a suit that fits well and has no doubt at least heard of Saville Row.
* He does not wear socks or underwear with cartoon characters on them – EVER. In fact, a true gentleman never really wears pink socks either; red, blue or colourful socks are fine, but never pink.

* He does not wear lycra, even if he's a cyclist. Sorry, but there ARE other options.
* You can never see the lining of his underwear or, God forbid, the crack of his manly regions upon sitting down or bending over.
* Shoes with laces, that aren't trainers, such as a classic pair of English Oxfords are an excellent sign, especially if they are buffed and in good condition.
* He certainly does not wear jeans that are tighter than yours.
* He does not leave his top button undone when wearing a tie but would always remove a tie with an open neck shirt.
* He makes the effort to wear a collared shirt and not a T-shirt when at any social gathering, even a gathering that happens during the day.
* He does not get told he looks like a celebrity because of any effort he makes to do so (unless it is purely effortless and coincidental).
* He has a subtle smell of cologne that accentuates his natural odour. Ideally dabbed in no more than two spots so he doesn't smell like he's fallen into an apothecary.
* He does not grow facial hair that makes him appear as if he's going through a midlife crisis, or that requires 'brushing'.
* He does not have gnawed fingers or fingernails.
* He doesn't wear a wedding ring – yes, it means he's married!

Choice of Accessories

* He carries an umbrella in the city but not in the country where there is an unwritten taboo against carrying an umbrella (unless of course they are with a lady who may potentially need shielding from the elements).
* If you see him with an iPad take notice of the case it's in and whether it reflects his style. Extra points if he appears to be reading the newspaper (points deducted if he is playing games of any description: you need a man not a boy).
* If you see him at the airport, he owns leather luggage or a travel bag.
* He sports cufflinks. Stylish designer cufflinks are always classy, but even if they are funny, it's actually a sign of his personality and are a great conversation starter.
* He wears a classic, quality watch to match his attire, nothing too flashy or showy but something suitable to the rest of his outfit.
* He does not wear more jewellery than you and certainly does not believe in 'bling'.
* He would never be seen dead wearing sunglasses indoors or to a wedding when wearing a suit.
* He knows his choice of wallet says a lot about his personality. Watch if he's carrying a bi-fold wallet in a classic colour or a quality card sleeve or money clip. Both options are equally fine.

* Extra points for a pocket square in the jacket breast pocket. However, it's important to note that never should a pocket square match a tie. Instead, they must complement each other – so he gets even more points if he gets that right.

If you have met him a couple of times

* He remembers your name when you see him again.
* He knows how to hold eye contact with you when he talks to you.
* He stands up to shake hands with you or when someone else walks into the room.
* He has impeccable speech. This matters not because of his background but because of his ambition. If he says things that put himself down or allude to his confidence you can hear it in his speech.
* He is humble and unassuming, and does not perceive himself to be better or worse than anyone else.
* He is highly regarded by his peers or colleagues.
* He is composed. You will never find a gentleman raising his voice, bragging about sexual conquests or getting into arguments.
* He is inclusive of you in group conversations when you don't know everyone.
* He makes you feel comfortable being around him without having to try too hard.
* He does not ignore you and pretend not to have seen you, but instead comfortably says hello with a smile.

On a first date:

* He doesn't take you to the cinema.
* He doesn't take you to a spa, pool or jacuzzi or anywhere else where you will have to de-clothe.
* He does not make you do anything that makes you sweat just to show you how much of a man he is.
* He considers the fact you may be wearing heels so will not suggest walking too far unless he's warned you in advance of what you'll need to wear.
* He helps you with your coat.
* He compliments you, extra points if he compliments one thing specifically such as your shoes or necklace.
* He is polite to waiters or bar staff, but at the same time is confident enough to be able to complain if something isn't right (nothing wrong with that if done politely, we shouldn't be embarrassed).
* He does not imply that he is very good at 'massages'.
* He asks more than you answer and knows how to keep conversation flowing. He certainly does not encourage awkward silences.
* He does not say, 'God I don't know how you can eat that' at dinner or comment on your menu choices.
* He does not look at his feet when he walks.
* He does not look at your chest when you talk.
* He is aware of his own body language and body odour.
* He does not use his mobile when talking to you, as it implies it is more important than you are, and he does not leave it on the table while you are eating.

* He does not show you YouTube videos while on a date. It's not that funny and is really quite awkward.
* He pays for the first few dates despite your kind offer to contribute.
* He does not invite the boys to come along later to show you how popular he is or because he's run out of interesting things to say.
* He has vision, he is driven and will not tell you stories of the last time he got drunk.

When you get to know him one-on-one

* He calls his family.
* He hugs his family.
* He does not call you 'babe'.
* He only has eyes for you when you are out together.
* He never makes reference to how 'hot' his ex-girlfriend was.
* He likes to read the newspaper and is up to date with current affairs.
* He is persuasive, not persistent.
* He makes reservations.
* He is confident and not arrogant.
* He keeps his word, and when he talks about another date he follows through.
* He might get drunk but will never be disorderly.
* He laughs heartily and not because he has to.
* He makes you laugh heartily and not because you have to.

* He takes care of other people as well as taking care of himself.
* You can get to the bottom of his passions.
* He is thoughtful and considerate and arranges the next date before the current one has ended or very soon after.
* He calls when he says he will.
* He can admit when he is wrong.
* He is cultured, well-travelled and educated about international affairs.
* He will not mock the success of others or blame others for his failings.
* He doesn't flash his cash and is aware of the financial situation of others around him.
* He sticks to his word.

Why men don't chat you up

In this Great country of ours, we often hear tales of how men from exotic foreign lands approach women. We hear how they are persistent, they are charming, how they effortlessly strike up conversation with strangers, and will happily walk up to a group of women without thinking about it too much because they simply *must* speak to them. We hear about how they firmly and resolutely ask women out on these things called 'dates', where they charm and romance their way into you spending time with them. We hear all this, and we sigh – half wondering with fascination how it must feel to be the object of one's attention so unquestionably, and the other half wondering why on earth we've never, as British women, felt we've experienced such blatant seduction from chaps Unlike other nations, British men do not feel empowered by their ability to romance you, but terrified. Unlike other nations British men do not feel masculine by their ability to win you over, only relieved that you didn't reject them! before. Apparently, it's called 'romancing' a lady, but to us Brits this can quite often feel like such an alien concept it almost warrants us to do the one thing we do so well – laugh.

In a quest to, therefore, try to understand why men are this way, we may resort to watching romantic comedies, or reading relationship advice books. However, these only set to confuse us further as they are, more often than not, American, and not relevant in the slightest to British behaviours, customs or reality. So much so, in fact, that we often end up questioning our ability to ever meet anyone nice. Ever. If we do start seeing a chap, our friends might advise us to follow the old mantras of 'play hard to get' or 'treat them mean to keep them keen' only to realise that we never really feel we get the balance quite right between being laid back and being too keen, never knowing what the chap you're seeing is responding well to. So how should we know how to play it?

This is because us Brits are not like any other nation. British men are not overtly comfortable with the concept of 'dating' or approaching women, as it only makes them feel vulnerable and uncomfortable. Unlike other nations, British men do not feel empowered by their ability to romance you, but terrified.

Unlike other nations, British men do not feel masculine by their ability to win you over, only relieved that you didn't reject them!

So when it comes to approaching women, they would simply, and quite remarkably, not bother. The reality, therefore, is that very rarely do men actually approach girls they like to 'chat up'.

There are several reasons for this. One of which is, as discussed, due to how us Brits are culturally. We are a pretty reserved and perhaps slightly non-communicative bunch in comparison with other nations, and we find it hard to open up until we feel we get to know each other quite well. It's simply not socially acceptable to strike up conversations with random strangers unless you have been introduced through friends or are under the influence of a bit of liquid courage. However, another crucial reason men do not approach women is because often the more they like you, the harder it is to actually even fathom saying anything to you. Yes that's right, the more a chap genuinely wants to get to know you, the less likely it is he will talk to you, chat you up or act in any way interested. It might sound really back to front but just think about it for a moment. When you see a really attractive chap, say at work or out with your friends, do you feel as confident talking to him as you would any of your other friends or acquaintances? You might suddenly feel a bit nervous and get butterflies in your stomach about the prospect of talking to him, when you are usually so confident and comfortable chatting to everyone else.

It's exactly the same for men. If they aren't really that interested (or only after one thing) you'll probably find they have absolutely no problem chatting to you, and they may well have tried their 'chat-up' approach to several girls before meeting you. If they genuinely are interested, however, they are much more likely to want to make a good impression, and they will be mindful of what they say, how they act and fundamentally how they make their move. This is why in Britain so many more romances happen after a few drinks as the alcohol infused guards come down and the confidence levels go up.

Where are they hiding?

I'm afraid to say, and I am going to try and break this to you gently, but much like there is no cookie-cutter definition of a gentleman, there are also no specific places where all gentlemen hang out regularly and congregate. In fact, good men are everywhere, and we as women need to be open to meeting them in as many places as possible. That being said, however, there are certain specific events, occasions or places that I do believe are more aplenty with chaps than others, so whilst you should absolutely be open to meeting people everywhere, here are some good places to start:

Sporting Occasions

We all know how men love to gather together to watch and play sport. There is something ever so primal about their love for it as it conjures up associations with the struggles for victory and the battles involved with winning and losing. Many men love to support a team almost more than they do a religion, and there is a certain notion that who they support says something about them as a person. I suspect too that inside almost every man is a somewhat 'never quite made it' sportsman, as it's probably every little boy's dream to become a successful athlete one day. I do seem to recall a few of my ex-boyfriends claiming they could have 'gone pro' had it not been for their knee injury or their height, when in reality it was probably more to do with their adolescence kicking in and discovering girls were suddenly far more interesting.

Sporting occasions, in general, are therefore great places to meet lots of chaps. But which specific ones should we be mindful of trying to attend? Let's take a look at some of our options.

Bars and Pubs

Generally speaking, there is a bit of an unwritten rule in Britain that the nicer the establishment you frequent, the better the quality of the clientele. Therefore, think carefully about where you're deciding to head out for those drinks with your girlfriends if you want to meet a quality sort. If you're heading to the same grotty, run-down pub because it's been your local for years, you may want to start venturing further afield. Also, try not to go back to the same place more than a couple of times when you're single, so you get into the habit of being open to new places and opportunities. We Brits do tend to enjoy knowing and frequenting our favourite places (such as the local pub) more often than we should because we more often than not prefer to opt for convenience and familiarity.

Be sure to consider also the layout and ambiance of the bars and pubs you go to. Ideally, you want somewhere loud enough to have atmosphere but quiet enough to be able to have a conversation so you can get chatting to people, and avoid bars and pubs with too many seated areas and not enough areas to mingle. Always try to position yourself near the hustle and bustle and never opt to sit at the back of the room straight away if you can avoid it.

Make sure you're mindful to frequent bars and pubs when there are key sports matches on. Even if you're not really into sport, it's definitely worth finding out what big sport matches are being televised and in which bars they are broadcasted, so you can head on down there and grab a good spot near the screen. You will be putting yourself directly in the line of vision of many a man, and will certainly get their attention. Just be sure it's not for the wrong reasons and that you and your friends don't start obstructing the view of the screen in any way. There's a difference by being strategically close to a screen and an obstruction to their viewing pleasure, so be careful!

If you do head out to a pub with a big group of friends, and perhaps some friends of friends who you don't know, be sure to introduce yourself to everyone. It's very rare for Brits to actually approach people cold to chat them up, as we'll explore later on, so it's often much easier, and much more socially acceptable, to have been introduced through mutual friends. So do try to make the effort to confidently say hello to as many people as you can so as to break the ice. Even if you don't find them your cup of tea, you never know which of their other friends may soon be arriving, so don't be shy about introducing yourself.

Private Member Clubs

If you live in a city or town where you have some private member clubs nearby, you might want to consider investigating membership. Often there is a perception that they are all really stuffy and expensive, and whilst this may be true for some of them, you might find one that suits your personality and budget. Often such clubs try to have members who share common interests, some being for creative people, others being for people who may work in finance and so on, so do some research before ruling them out as you could be missing a great opportunity to meet like-minded people. If you would like to join and need to be referred by some existing members (as is often the case with such clubs), then ask around in your network. You might be surprised to find you already have some friends who are members and who wouldn't mind referring you.

Nightclubs

Nightclubs have quite a bad reputation for places where you only meet rather questionable characters who are only after one thing. This is often the case, but, should you be inclined to go to a nightclub of any sort, it doesn't hurt to be selective about the type you frequent. In my humble opinion, nightclubs that lead downstairs should, where possible, be avoided (especially if you live in London) as more often than not they are tiny, dark, windowless rooms which can seem quite claustrophobic and questionably odorous. I always think that, if you can help it, you're much better off going to nightclubs which are located upstairs or on the same level as the entrance. These are usually infinitely more pleasant, and you'll often find a nicer crowd. That aside, however, if you find yourself going to a nightclub of any description, be aware of where you position yourself. Sticking close to the bar or the dance floor makes it much easier to mingle, and it doesn't hurt to befriend the bar staff and bouncers. Introduce yourself politely to people at the door if you get the chance and ask for their name, so they remember you the next time. You never know when it might come in handy.

Sports Clubs

It's generally a good idea to make the most of the area in which you live as you never know which nice chaps could be local to you already. Therefore, if you join your local tennis club, health club or even pony club, you will be finding like-minded individuals who share a common interest to you. What's more, meeting individuals in this manner is considered to Brits to be far less embarrassing than being picked up in a bar or any other place where it's quite so blatantly obvious that you're searching for a nice chap. Look up sports or hobby clubs that are local to you. Even if you don't have much interest in the sport (and let's face it, not everyone does) you can often still join some of these clubs as what's known as a 'Social Member'. This means you can join to use the café, bar and will get invited to all the annual balls and 'dos' without having to ever actually play the sport. This works particularly well for the slightly older generation or for people who live out in the country who want to take the initiative to connect to their local community in a reserved fashion.

Use your network

Often the best way of meeting new people in Britain is to make the most of the people you know. I know several people in my network who are always setting up their friends on dates with other friends, similarly to how I started out. If you know of anyone who loves to do a bit of matchmaking, then be sure to tell them that you're looking to meet someone nice. A lot of the time us Brits don't like to remind our friends we are proactively looking for anyone as we feel we're reinforcing to the world the fact that we are still single, which all seems so embarrassing. Don't be shy about asking your friends if they know of any nice chaps and certainly don't be embarrassed. We often take the same attitude to dating as we do to complaining in restaurants: we'd rather not bring it up as it makes us feel awkward. Don't be afraid to be direct and take the bull by the proverbial horns when looking for a nice chap. Spread the word, and you never know who you may get introduced to.

Also, if you're a social media user, get onto Facebook and Twitter and start being more proactive in posting if you're not already. The more you post, the more you'll pop up on other people's newsfeeds and you never know which of your friends may be interested in you, or have friends who are. Make your profile picture as good as it can be too, as often your kind friends might try to match you up with some of their single friends and the first thing they'll do is look you up on Facebook.

Online Dating

Online dating in Britain has become so commonplace that these days the stigma that was previously associated with couples who have met online really has dissipated into oblivion. In fact it is, on the whole, more often than not considered to be an incredibly efficient way to find a suitable partner as it doesn't require waiting for things to happen. Because the Brits are especially backward in coming forward when it comes to romancing a potential partner, they have zealously adopted the online dating world. It inevitably enables them to hide behind the computer and mask their humiliation in asking someone out or admitting they find someone attractive – which they often find so hard to do in person.

According to a study conducted by eHarmony and compiled by the Future Foundation, in 2014 27% of couples met online in the UK, with that figure expected to rise to 50% in 2031. It was also found in the same study that only 8% of people who met online got divorced or separated, so despite those horror stories we hear of people lying on their profile, or not looking anything like their profile picture, there is proof that it works.

If you haven't dipped your toe into the online dating pool, I would strongly urge you to give it a try, as you do get a sense of what is out there that you may be suited to. It also never hurts to go on a few practice dates with people you meet online, too, so you can learn to hone your dating skills and build your confidence. The problem with online dating though, in my opinion, is that the dating pool of people is often so large that a lot of people think there must constantly be something better out there. As a result, they tend not to settle on one person for long. It has consequently brought about many more serial daters than I think ever existed before.

There's also the fact that nobody has to answer to anyone they meet online. They are not referred by friends or family, or connected in the least to a social network. Therefore, the behaviour of those involved can be sometimes questionable. I often hear stories about men and women who would normally be upstanding individuals behaving in the most intolerable manner, so I do often wonder whether it brings out the best in people's character.

That being said, I would always encourage everyone to at least give it a go. If you do though, make sure you spend time writing a witty profile and getting some fabulous pictures taken. If you can afford to get some professional photos (including one full-length shot), it will be incredibly worthwhile. Men are terribly visual creatures so this will no doubt make a huge difference to how many get in touch. Should you be questioning joining an online dating site and don't know which one to join, it's very much a personal thing based upon your preferences. However, I personally believe that if you join one where you have to pay a monthly fee, you do meet a slightly better calibre of people. Many Brits I speak to often feel as though if they are paying for it they are deemed more desperate in some way than if they had managed to find love without the price tag. I couldn't disagree more. Not only are people willing to pay a small monthly fee more likely to be taking their relationship search seriously, but they are also unlikely to be a cheapskate – so consider yourself speculating to accumulate when choosing which online dating site is for you.

Matchmakers

With the vast surge in the amount of people dating online, and more recently dating on apps, there does seem to be this huge pool full of, what seem to be from the outset, potential fish.

Whilst a lot of people revel in being able to filter through endless photos of possible candidates, tirelessly writing to each one, many simply do not have the time nor the inclination to do so. They are simply far too busy to follow up with the conversations and go on date after date hoping to meet someone suitable to them, or they have tried it and have grown tired of the process. Often online dating can lead to nothing but inflated disappointment that, despite all the volume of candidates, they still haven't' met anyone they click with. This is one of the many reasons why people are now seeing too much choice as a negative thing and are turning to professional matchmakers to help them find their needle in the dating haystack. Some people also feel that online dating is just far too indiscreet and worry that friends or colleagues might see them on there, so they would rather opt for more understated ways of meeting their potential partner.

Matchmakers work specifically on behalf of their clients to find them someone they will be perfectly suited to, so they save huge amounts of time and effort for those involved. They also do any pre-screening necessary to ensure not just that you are compatible on multiple levels, but that they are who they say they are so there won't be any unwanted surprises. Anyone can hire a matchmaker, but some may be put off by the investment, as it's generally a more considered one. However be mindful that a stable relationship is one of the most important things in your life, so it's often far more worthwhile using your time efficiently and leaving it to the professionals to find someone for you. Also, as ladies, some matchmakers do let you join their books for free, or for a nominal charge. My matchmaking agency 'The Sloane Arranger' charges paying members who want me to work on their behalf, but I have a 'Little Black Book' full of eligible singles who can simply join for free. Should I have a paying member looking for someone like them, I then contact them. So be sure to look into matchmakers in your area and find out whether they are looking for people like you for their existing members. They might well be.

Dating Apps

In recent years, there's certainly been a growth in the use of dating apps that are somehow regarded as less time intensive than online dating. Instead of having to create a witty profile, or reply to people trying to be witty, you can simply let your picture do the talking and hope for the best. Some of these apps find people who are located in a certain radius to you, and others let you find people who you may have crossed paths with on your way to work. In theory, it's all about opening up the possibility to meeting new people without it being deemed too 'cringe-worthy' and awkward. To Brits this is ideal. In fact, it's somehow more socially acceptable to talk about going out with someone from Tinder than it is from an online dating site – even though there's not really that much difference between the two.

The fact that you needn't make any effort in writing a dating profile somehow denotes how desperate you are to finding love, so it's somehow given a silent nod of approval from the Brits. You might only tell your really close friends that you're giving online dating a go, but you really wouldn't mind sharing with anyone who will listen the fact that you're on Tinder, and probably even offer to let a few of your friends swipe left or right on your behalf (Oh the hours of fun!). The ironic thing is that these 'Dating App' are often so depressing. All dates that come out of them are based purely on physical attributes and so it's no wonder that the men on there are looking for only one thing. I despair sometimes when I meet women who come to me wondering why a relationship never materialised into anything serious from a dating app. If you want to use them, fine, go ahead, you never know you might meet someone nice, but my general advice would be, more often than not, don't expect the men on there to be quality chaps looking for a long term relationship. You have been warned.

Be wary too of thinking that you're saving time by using dating apps. I have spoken to several people who wistfully while away the time swiping one way or the other, and never actually meeting up with anyone. Isn't your time better spent actually meeting people than simply looking at photo after photo on your phone?

The Modern British Season

Whilst the modern British Season is no longer like it once was, certain customs and traditions have graciously (or ungraciously, depending upon the occasion) stood the test of time and are still firmly engrained within the British calendar. Often these are great excuses for groups of friends to have social gatherings in what they hope will be sunshine, and atmosphere, whilst getting rather donned up in their finest regalia.

These occasions can be fabulous opportunities to meet people, as often large groups attend these affairs en masse. However, it does take a certain amount of organisation and up front planning to do them properly, as often there are certain requirements that need to be adhered to in order to be able to access all areas. Furthermore, there are not just bureaucratic restrictions, but etiquette and dress code limitations too, and often if you're incorrectly attired you won't be allowed inside where you want to be.

It would be remiss of me not to mention that some of today's traditionally elegant events have now achieved what can only be deemed a tarnished reputation. Not a year goes by when the papers don't print stories about the increasingly orange, the occasionally shoeless and the consistently drunk attendees to Cheltenham or Ascot (or 'Chavscot', as it's often now referred to), and it is for this reason that I must stress that if you do plan to attend such events, there are ways to do them in a more refined manner. I strongly urge you, therefore, not to partake in giving such events a tarnished reputation by bending the dress code rules or getting so drunk that you forget where you left your shoes or how to get home. Not only will this do you no favours in your quest to finding a nice chap, but you will undoubtedly feel pretty rotten the next day too.

What a Lovely Lady Can Do About It

Getting a nice chap starts with YOU

Embody Eligibility

Embodying eligibility is a guiding set of principles for the classy and refined modern lady. Out with antiquated, old fashioned mantras that teach us how to ignore men to get them interested, 'Walk like you have three men walking behind you' Oscar De La Renta

how to treat them mean to keep them keen, how to understand how they think and respond accordingly. We are not here to tiptoe around men and try to decode their thoughts. I believe we deserve better, so we need to be presenting ourselves with our highest heel forwards.

Women today are hugely pressured to be able to do everything. Get a job, be successful, be a mother, be a wife, be a friend, pay the bills – and we strive to balance it all as best as we can, more often than not incredibly well. However, due to our in-built biology, we only have a certain window of time to do some of these things, and so there is often even more pressure after we reach a certain age to find ourselves a nice chap and start popping out some babies. A lot of women therefore start to feel that there is something fundamentally wrong with them if they have failed to do this for whatever reason. Women in their mid-30s and beyond can often start to lose confidence in themselves, and they gradually start to feel the power they previously had over men in their 20s slowly shifting away as younger, prettier models are seemingly ever present.

Camilla, a beautiful and charming friend of mine, was going through something very similar. Well educated, a chiropodist and with a fabulous sense of style, she came to see me after she had been to four of her friends' weddings over one summer and each time was sat on a 'singles' table'. Although undoubtedly happy for her dear friends, she couldn't mask her true feelings after a while. She also couldn't take the pitying looks of sympathy from her friends and their families – or the inevitable comments such as 'oh not to worry! You'll find a nice guy soon'. When we delved into it, it wasn't because these singles' tables didn't have nice people on them. Sure, perhaps they weren't all her cup of tea, but she did say there were a few she found attractive. It was predominantly because Camilla was starting to doubt herself so much she stopped exuding 'eligibility' and wouldn't feel comfortable striking up conversation with people for fear of not coming across well. Previously the life and soul in her twenties, she became so much more insecure and less confident about her ability to successfully appeal to a man. When a guy would show interest and begin texting her she painstakingly analysed each text, carefully calculating when to respond and what to say, often asking all her friends for their thoughts before pressing send.

Unfortunately, when women don't embody 'eligibility', quality men often pick up on these signals of worry or 'trying too hard' to please, and will simply not respond positively. Rather than being intrigued by their mystery or attracted by their charm, they will sense they are needy or insecure and will let the woman be the one who becomes more interested in them. What you tend to find in instances like these is therefore that the men get turned off and the women end up hooking up with anyone just to make themselves feel better and prove to themselves they've 'still got it'. Unfortunately, going home with a guy too soon, as we all know, more often than not leads to nowhere as it hasn't allowed for enough time for the chap to build up that intrigue and mystery that will make you so valuable to him.

'Eligibility' is caring more about yourself than what others think of you. It's about being kind to yourself because you're fabulous, appreciating and valuing yourself and not worrying about what he thinks or what his opinions are. The moment you start trying to work out what other people want, the less time you spend working out what is important to *you*. Have you ever noticed how often the most eligible, charming people you meet can often be the most strongly opinionated and forthright in their view of the world? It's because they really don't care what others think of them and people love and respect them for it (more often than not). It's not always so for the people who are self-conscious or constantly aware of how their opinions will be perceived. These people often strive to fit in and struggle, when those who really don't care could probably be placed in almost every social situation without batting an eyelid. You weren't born to be like somebody else, you were created unique so embrace yourself and be proud of your opinion and your outlook on life.

Embodying 'Eligibility' is about trying to get yourself looking and feeling as good about yourself as you can be; it is about ensuring you are morally doing what is right, that you are leading with your most charmingly funny and attractive feet first and that you are great at breaking the ice and holding your own. It is about being independent, self-sufficient, correct and refined, and being as attractive as you can be as a person, both physically and mentally.

I think a lot of women today unfortunately make the mistake of seeking to stand out in the wrong ways. They are outlandishly loud, or dress provocatively in a bid to get attention and lead more with their sexuality than their charisma. Armani once famously quoted that 'Elegance is not about being noticed, it's about being remembered' and I couldn't agree more.

Don't lead with your sexuality, lead with your elegance

Now this one is an obvious one but one I repeatedly find myself advising my clients. Less is very much more when it comes to finding yourself your handsome partner. Now don't get me wrong, there's nothing wrong with showing a bit of skin and you should absolutely dress to accentuate your killer assets, but when people say dress 'sexy' I always wish I could replace that word with 'elegant'.

Armani once famously quoted that 'Elegance is not about being noticed, it's about being remembered,' and I couldn't agree more.

The mistake women often make is that they dress far too

provocatively in order to get attention and to fundamentally boost their own ego, as they love the attention it generates. They might wear short skirts and put their flesh on display, as they prefer to feel desirable and get men looking at them over merely blending into a crowd. This is especially true in Britain where men don't really chat women up, so male attention is considered the next best thing to an approach in some cases. It's simply much more of an ego boost to have had some attention than to go home and feel as though you were pretty much invisible the whole night. Now, whilst it's fully understandable that nobody likes to feel like part of the furniture, some women really do take things too far. They wrongly think that dressing to show it all off will make men find them more attractive, but in reality the type of guy who's going to go for the super-sexy dresser will only be motivated by one thing. Yup, you guessed it! Most charming chaps I know who are looking for a serious relationship would rather date someone they could be proud to show off to their friends, family and colleagues, and more often than not that is the more elegant, demure lady who doesn't need to show it all off physically as she's got an awful lot more to offer than just her appearance.

The next time you are going out with your friends and contemplating what to wear, have an honest look at how you think you're coming across. It's fine to show off legs _or_ breasts _or_ arms but if you're overdoing it you might be giving off the wrong signals. Besides, you want to leave more to the imagination. Otherwise you're simply giving away too much too soon, and we all know how much men love a bit of intrigue.

If you think this sounds tricky and perhaps you have a group of friends who all dress to 'impress' (so to speak), and you don't want to feel like the odd one out, it's important to note that I'm not suggesting in the slightest you seek to become unattractive or play down what God gave you. I'm just suggesting you choose to make elegant choices over sexy ones. You might actually be surprised the different kind of attention you receive. Also, if your friends continue to dress provocatively, remember that it's not a competition. Often women dress not just to impress men, but to impress other women too – so don't try to outdo each other in the sexy-stakes. More often than not, you'll only stand out for the wrong reasons.

Sexy	-	Wearing clothes that are fashionable now but in a few years you'll find a photo of yourself and cringe whilst screaming 'what was I thinking?'
Elegant	-	Wearing classic items that look good on you effortlessly, regardless of trends.
Sexy	-	Dressing to show it all off. Showing breasts and legs and anything else going.
Elegant	-	Dressing to leave something to the imagination. Showing either breasts or legs (and never both) in an understated and demure fashion.
Sexy	-	Accessories include your phone, bracelets, earrings, watches, necklaces or any other jewellery that you can find.
Elegant	-	Accessories are your personality: gloves,

		scarves hats, belts, handbags and jewellery that say something about you and define you.
Sexy	-	Being provocative with a guy, flirting outrageously and making sure he notices you. Relying on your appearance to help you stand out.
Elegant	-	Being interesting and having something to say for yourself. Looking fabulous yes, but you have far more to offer than just your appearance alone.
Sexy	-	Changing your hairstyle to follow trends. You might love the recent haircut of a celebrity and try to emulate it.
Elegant	-	You know how your hair suits you and wouldn't dream of copying anyone else.

www.sovainbooks.co.uk/elegantsexy

Find your Elegance

If you're not entirely sure what your elegance is yet, perhaps you tend to wear safe and comfortable clothes, or perhaps you're not really into hair and makeup or just don't think you have the time to faff about with it all. Well, my advice would be, if you're serious about finding someone special, you need to put time into making yourself the best version of yourself you can be. Now is the very best time to maximise your potential and to look and feel as good as you can about yourself. So if you're not getting your hair done professionally now, you never will, and if you're not putting a little makeup on to bring out your gorgeous face, then you never will. And if you're not giving yourself your own 'wow factor', ask yourself why you're not. You might think you'd only like to meet a guy who takes you as you are, 'au natural'. Whilst this may be true (a lot of guys aren't into heavily made-up faces), there's no reason why you can't put a little something on to accentuate what you've got.

A gorgeous blonde friend of mine, Lucinda, was a perfect example of someone who needed to find her elegance. A dancer with an absolute killer body, she would always look amazing in whatever she wore and loved to get dressed up in fabulous outfits with great makeup to match. The only thing was that she would always wash her hair and then just leave it to dry naturally, so it would hang wet around her shoulders. She was one of those wash-and-go kind of girls I know many women would truly envy. She popped in to see me on the way to one of her dates (a second date with a guy she really liked) and I literally had to walk her to the nearby hairdressers and insisted she get her hair blow-dried professionally. The reason she never actually dried her hair was purely because she never got into the habit of it as her hair always dried naturally straight, but a good blow dry works wonders. Not only did it give her a bit more 'va va voom' and she looked amazing, but she felt like a movie star and exuded such confidence and sass like never before. Suddenly every head movement was an opportunity to shine (literally)!

When you're single, every day and every situation is a potential opportunity to meet someone new. Imagine you're on your way to work and you see the man of your dreams! Wouldn't you wish you'd looked your best then? Men are very visual, as I already mentioned, and they really do respond better to visual cues. So make the most of yourself and find your elegance. Not just for them, but for yourself too, as the more fabulous you look, the more fabulous you will feel and you will ooze eligibility and confidence like never before.

So whilst you're in the mode of introspection, have a root around your wardrobe and be honest with yourself. Do you need fewer baggy clothes? Do you find you wear the same things all the time? Are you choosing to dress comfortably over stylishly? Take this opportunity to refresh your wardrobe, improve your exercise routine, get your nails done, get a new haircut and buy some fabulous heels and accessories that accentuate both your look and your personality.

I once had a client named Georgie who was in her late 30s, and although she was incredibly attractive, after her divorce she found herself wearing an awful lot of black. 'I just seem to have found myself in a rut' she told me one day 'and a large amount of what I end up wearing is very samey'. On a subconscious level Georgie was mourning the end of her marriage and she was keen to mask her insecurity and hurt by wearing black and comfortable clothes rather than vibrant, stylish outfits that suited her an awful lot more. I knew that if she had come to me and was ready to find love, she was ready to make some changes, so one day I took her shopping along with one of my stylists and we totally transformed her wardrobe. We avoided anything too garish, but instead found her simple, elegant items such as classic silk shirts and scarves, which spruced things up incredibly well. It's amazing the colour that comes back into the cheeks and the glint in the eyes that appears when someone feels good about themselves. She also found a brand new lease of confidence, and it had a notable impact on her dating life. The better she felt, the better she came across.

We, as women, have fundamentally changed our style cues over the decades. Back in the 19th century, we would have taken cues on how to dress and present ourselves from the royal family or the royal court, but today there are a whole host of role models or style advocates appealing to a very wide range of ages. These can be anything from glamour models, to reality TV stars, famous actresses or fashion models. This can lead to a lot of misinterpretation in terms of what is 'elegant'. This, coupled with the growth of the 'fast-food' shopping culture, has enabled us to be more experimental with our style without the expense. However, what is in fashion doesn't necessarily correspond to what is elegant and it won't always look good on you, so shop to suit your own look/personality and don't worry too much about what's currently in vogue.

Some top tips to finding your elegance:

* Find your style and stick to it. Elegance comes from discovering your personal style and knowing exactly what suits you.
* Invest in accessories just as much as you do in your clothes. Shoes, handbags, gloves, scarves and jewellery can make a modest outfit appear triple the value.
* Stick to the etiquette of elegance: alligator shoes or bags should only be worn for sport or travel and certainly not for the evening, never wear white shoes (unless one lives in Essex or is getting married) and avoid white handbags unless you're going somewhere hot.
* Recognise your investment pieces: buy a good pair of jeans, black trousers and a solid coat.
* Don't wear jewellery that ages you. Pearl earrings may be for your mother but they are probably not best suited if you're under 50.
* Recognise there is a difference between fashion and style. Never wear anything because it looks good on someone else, but instead think of your outfit as a way to represent the best version of yourself.
* Always consider how your outfits will look when you're sitting down and avoid really narrow skirts that have a tendency to ride up.

There's a time and place for every outfit

Whilst it's important to dress elegantly rather than sexily, it's also crucial to try not to let your appearance act as a barrier to connecting with people, and it's important to recognise there is a time and place for every outfit. Your appearance should fundamentally reflect your style and personality, but just be mindful of overdressing at inopportune moments too. Very often gorgeous women will feel empowered by fantastic clothes and quite rightly so. They will embody eligibility as they should and they will go out and buy expensive handbags, scarves and jewellery, and look absolutely stunning and well put together. Now, whilst there is nothing wrong with this, it's certainly good to consider that if you're appearing too overdressed you might be putting people off. Your appearance, in fact, does actually play a really large role in either helping or hindering your approachability. It's a dramatic example, but imagine you were donned head to toe in diamonds (some of you might quite like that idea); how many men do you think would really feel comfortable talking to you? It's hard enough as it is in the UK without extra appearance barriers.

Now, I'm not saying you should dress down, but just be mindful of what you're choosing to wear and when, as what you want is to make sure you open yourself up to as many opportunities to meet new people as possible.

A good example of why is when I set up a male member of my agency, Oscar, with a gorgeous girl, Lilly. They had a huge amount in common, went to the same university, lived in the same part of London, and when I showed them both photos of each other they were really enthusiastic about the date. I had a coffee with Lilly before the date as I always do, and gave her a bit more background on Oscar. She seemed so pleased and excited and left the coffee jovially commenting 'oh what is a girl to wear?' Having dressed beautifully on every occasion I had met her, I told her not to venture into territory too dissimilar to her typical style as she always looked lovely. Lilly, unfortunately, got a little too excited and ended up putting perhaps a bit too much effort for a casual drink in a pub in Fulham. For a cold November afternoon, she turned up wearing a rather short, emerald green satin evening dress with heels that looked like she was on her way to a ball after her date with Oscar.

After the date, I caught up with Oscar, and while he had a great time and thought Lilly was a beautiful girl, he did admit that he felt slightly overwhelmed by her choice of outfit, especially as he came straight from work wearing jeans and a shirt. He didn't really feel he could feel comfortable. 'I just didn't know what to say to her' he told me.

Work out what you want

Leave your baggage at the door

If you're serious about making love happen for you, you need to take some time and think about what has been holding you back. It's time to make a decision to let go of anything that's been preventing you from moving forward and to be completely honest with yourself. Why is it that you don't think you've found the one? Or maybe you did find him and he hurt you? More often than not we have baggage that prevents us from opening up to someone new, or we are scared of rejection. Perhaps you are afraid of dating as it all seems really awkward or you're in a mindset where you just want to give up. Perhaps you've been doing online dating for just too long and have gone on one too many disappointing dates you can't see the effort=reward ratio playing in your favour.

The best thing you can do if you're at this point is to have a little break from dating and enjoy your own company for a while. Stop dating completely for a couple of months and focus on what is important to you. Go to the gym, get fit, take a cookery course, spend some time with your family and friends and just enjoy yourself. Do all the things that you never found time to do when you were in a relationship as there was always someone else to consider. Now is your time to be truly selfish and do what you please. Cleanse any negative feeling with positive action and be really kind to yourself for a while. Without sounding too 'new age', you do need to give yourself a bit of love every now and then and you shouldn't feel bad in the slightest for doing so. In fact, the more you learn to love yourself, the more someone else will realise how amazing you are and love you back.

Throw away your superficial list

Many women carry around subconscious (or often conscious) lists that they may have created when they were 17 of what their ideal man must be like and, unfortunately, rule out lots of potentially lovely men right from the start. These lists generally include pretty superficial things such as 'he must be over 6ft', 'he must have brown hair' or 'he must look like a cross between Brad Pitt and Henry Cavill in the looks department with the charm of Hugh Grant'. If you're guilty of such, it's absolutely crucial that you throw away lists you may have created if you're serious about finding someone special as all these do is hold you back. So many times when I ask clients what it is they are looking for, they reel off a list of physical or impractical attributes that are simply unrealistic in the modern world. Furthermore, often there is a great deal of hesitancy and inflexibility to change these long-standing perceptions of what their perfect man means to them.

Whilst I'm not saying we should settle for anything less than we deserve, we must be realistic in what we're aiming to achieve, and we must recognise that our definition of 'perfect' may change as we get older. I know when I was sixteen my perfect man was Leonardo DiCaprio, but I'm pretty sure we'd not be quite so suited now. Furthermore, I know from my many years matchmaking that there is no perfect guy. The ideal man who lives on so many a woman's list simply does not exist in real life. Whilst that may be disappointing for several of you to hear, I do know one thing which may be of some consolation, and that is there is undoubtedly a perfect guy for *you*. He just might not be perfect in the way you had envisaged him being on that list that you wrote when you were younger. What's more, if you keep on looking for what's on the list you'll never truly appreciate the wonderful men you may actually meet and cross paths with in your life.

Please do yourselves a favour and stop looking down at those lists and start to look up at what's around you. You might be surprised at who you meet or who you have chemistry with at the most unexpected moments.

What are your core relationship drivers?

Whilst it's important that you throw away any superficial lists of what your perfect man means to you, you do need to spend a bit of time working out what your fundamental and core relationship drivers are. These are key make or break factors that define who you are as a person and who you could be compatible with. Unlike a list of how tall or handsome a chap should be, these drivers look at what is absolutely essential for you to have from a partner in order to be happy and fulfilled in both the near and distant future.

Unfortunately, when it comes down to it, a lot of relationships fundamentally fail because both or either party never really knew what they were looking for when they got involved to begin with. A relationship is like anything else in life that we strive to achieve, and it really does help to have a goal and idea for what you want out of it, before getting into it. Therefore, taking the time to work out and prioritise what factors you consider to be top of your relationship scale may save you a lot of time and heartache in the long run if you really think about what you're looking for. It's also a great exercise as it gets you to visualise a goal more clearly, and oddly enough, often the more we visualise what we want from life, the more it has a funny way of presenting itself to us.

Consider for a moment the relationship values below and mark out of 10 (10 being the highest score) how important each one of these are to you.

	Score		Score		Score
Ambition That he's a go-getter with a vision		**Authenticity** What you see is what you get		**Background** That he has a similar background, education, religion	

Attraction That he is physically attractive		Security That the relationship is safe and comfortable		Stability That the relationship is stable	
Commitment That he will be committed to the relationship		Financial That he has a sound financial background		Fidelity That he will be faithful	
Future That he wants the same things as me: children, retirement, etc.		Humour That he can make me laugh when I don't feel like smiling		Integrity That he's a good person, with a sound moral compass	
Intellect That he challenges himself and me intel-lectually		Passion That you can get to the core of what drives him		Positivity That he is optimistic	

Identifying your relationship drivers, and really thinking about them, will be hugely instrumental in enabling you to build better relationships. I'll sometimes get phone calls from my clients after they've been dating for a few months telling me it hasn't worked out, and more often than not it's because some fundamental values have surfaced further down the line that weren't identified to begin with.

It's important to be true to yourself when you do these charts though. A great example for why reminds me of John, a charming finance guy from Wimbledon, who came to see me two years after he'd gone through a divorce. He was a great guy, very good looking, with a good job, and after dating a few girls here and there, he was on the lookout for a serious relationship. When I first met him I tried to get to the bottom of his values and find out what he was looking for, and he mentioned that his ex-wife was unfaithful so he really wanted someone loyal, as he just couldn't take the lies and the mistrust that he had experienced before. Taking this on board, I took it upon myself to find John a really great girl, who valued fidelity and integrity just as much as he did. After a few dates, I introduced him to a very glamorous and independent woman called Hettie, and they seemed to hit it off. Three dates turned to four and after several months they were a self-deemed couple. I was so delighted and so was John, until a few months later when Hettie called me out of the blue in tears telling me all about how she found out John was seeing other women the entire time they were dating. How did she find out? Text messages suddenly appeared on his phone and she read perhaps more than he would have liked. Basically, what happened with John was that he wasn't honest with himself about what he was looking for and what his priorities were when we met. What he told me was that he wanted a committed relationship from a loyal partner, but in reality, he wasn't ready for that and after his divorce what he really wanted was to have a bit of fun. Therefore, just be completely honest when you do this exercise, as otherwise the only person you're cheating on is yourself and you're just going to end up hurting people and feeling pretty rubbish about it.

Once you have worked out your priorities, take a moment to think about whether your past relationships have been aligned with them. Is there a big gap between what matters to you and the type of guy you've been dating in the past? If so, it might be worth re-evaluating what you should be looking for going forward and trying not to get too involved with a guy who doesn't correlate to your core relationship needs.

Be Open Minded

Be less mistrusting of strangers

A big part of our British culture leads to us being more reserved than our European neighbours. We don't tend to have our hearts on our sleeves all that often as a nation, and we usually prefer to wait until we have known someone for a good couple of years before we welcome them into our select circle of friends.

This means we can often find it pretty much socially unacceptable to strike up conversation with strangers anywhere other than out socialising in a bar or restaurant (and only then generally mentioning social niceties), so any introduction that goes outside of this very narrow spectrum of acceptability is regarded with a certain amount of mistrust. It doesn't matter whether you're from Britain or not, breaking the ice with a Brit can often feel like a wobbly bridge: nobody knows whether it will be crossed without someone plummeting over the edge.

But why so? Do we all get swathes of anxiety if someone talks to us? I doubt it. We talk to people all the time when ordering food at restaurants or making friends with the person who serves us our coffee in the morning. These are strangers too, but on the whole, when it comes to making new friends and having a relationship, we can be terribly mistrusting of strangers.

It's somehow 'OK' if a stranger is introduced via a mutual friend, they are the subconscious seal of approval and welcomed into the group more readily than complete strangers, but even then you very rarely find a great deal of effort made from existing friends to get to know this new stranger. This reminds me of how we used to behave when a new girl joined our class at school: everyone would leave her to it for the first few days and suss her out until we felt confident enough to start getting to know her. It's exactly the same with a new friend welcomed into the group. Very often, unless they have natural gravitas and charming conversation, the new friend can be made to feel like they are constantly 'missing the joke' or not quite riding the frequency wave of the conversation. Furthermore, very rarely does anyone ask about this new stranger directly to try to get to know them. They are simply accepted into the group but it's not expected that they would be considered a permanent fixture until they have met several times.

Have a think about it. When was the last time you met someone new, perhaps a friend that a friend of yours brought along? Did you really ask them questions about themselves and try to get to know them? It's amazing how opportunities to meet new people come about from every person you meet, so be sure to take an interest in new people, ask them questions about themselves, and be proactive about making a concerted effort. They will no doubt find you incredibly charming, and you might also feel really good about yourself.

Whilst it's slightly easier for friends of friends, the infiltration process for complete strangers to social groups can often be much harder, and take a certain amount than by simply having mutual friends in common. But if someone starts talking to you randomly, especially a chap who could be a potential love interest – embrace it. We should be trying to encourage and welcome people who have the confidence to chat rather than punishing them by being totally mistrusting. Besides, the more people you know and the more friends you make, whether they may be permanent friends or friends you hang out with for a short period of time (who might introduce you to new people), the more likely it is to get introduced to new men, so be open to increasing your network as much as you can.

Be a 'Yes Person'

It's not just about being more open to meeting and mingling with strangers that is key to increasing your social network, but it's also about being open generally to every single potential *opportunity* that comes your way. It's what I call being a 'Yes Person' and I swear by this concept as I have tried it myself, and it really does work.

When I broke up with one of my ex-boyfriends years ago, I, like many of us, was feeling a little bit sorry for myself. I didn't feel like doing much and kept finding myself opting for a night in in favour of getting dressed up to go out. On the few occasions I did go out, I'd find myself surrounded by couples and this only seemed to make me feel worse. One of my friends had noticed my slump in energy and lack of interest in things I would previously have jumped at the chance to do – and she suggested I try being a 'Yes Person' for one month as a challenge to myself. She had done it herself too when she was going through a rough patch and found it hugely eye opening how many opportunities came her way that she would never have imagined. More often than not we are creatures of habit, and we like to go to places we're familiar with or go out with people we feel comfortable around, but if you challenge these conventions in your mind you might be surprised by what comes your way.

The concept is incredibly simple; for one month just say yes to every opportunity, event, occasion, invitation or suggestion that comes your way. Obviously we don't have to say yes to absolutely everything, so if a chap asks you to go home with him on a first date then that's not what we're talking about (more on that later). However, if you find yourself at work and some colleagues are going for a quick glass of wine at the end of the day and you'd usually find yourself turning down the invitation, why not go for it? You never know who might be there. Similarly, if you have been invited to a birthday party of a friend that you don't know all that well, don't be shy, go along! Make the most of everything that comes your way (at least for a short period of time) and see how the universe finds a way of opening up opportunities to you.

www.sovainbooks.co.uk/yesperson

Don't Hold Yourself Back

Stop saying sorry

Why oh why do we insist on apologising for everything? It's frankly quite disconcerting how much women over-apologise for things these days. Although, it must be said: it's a rather British quirk. We've all been there - and I too, am often found guilty of this unnecessary trait. You go out for dinner and the waiter gets your order wrong, or you're on the tube and someone brushes against you and invades your personal space – it's 'oh I'm terribly sorry'. We apologise profusely and continuously for things that quite frankly, just aren't our fault.

Studies have shown there are notably more women than men who are guilty of over-zealously using the word and it doesn't surprise me in the slightest. In fact, we've almost found ourselves mistakenly using the word 'sorry' as a form of politeness, of humbly making people like us, and as a replacement for 'excuse me' or 'pardon'. In fact, we use it almost as automatically as 'hello' and 'goodbye'.

So why is there such a big gender difference here? Why do we not find men doing this as much? Well, men, unlike women, are inherently more

For many British people... it is considered quite normal for the victim to mutter 'sorry'. This is clearly illogical, but for many British people it is an ingrained response Debretts.com* likely to not want to appear weak, and therefore, the more you apologise the more you are saying that you aren't all that confident, that you are ill at ease with yourself and that you are putting the person you are apologising to above yourself.

When dating, we've already discussed the importance of exuding eligibility, but how on earth can one appear fully confident, articulate and in control if they are apologising over minute details. There's nothing wrong with being polite, but be sure to try to check your use of the word 'sorry' when you really mean other things.

What to do if you're guilty of doing this:

* Make a note of how many times you say sorry in one day. If you're acutely aware of it you are much more likely to do something about it.
* Once you've recognised how much you use the word, challenge yourself not to say sorry at all for one day.
* Find replacement words. Say thank you instead for example. So if you're late for a date try putting an apology on its head by saying instead 'thank you so much for your patience' or 'thanks for waiting'.
* Try to work out why you're apologising. Is it just a habit or are you feeling insecure and starting to doubt yourself or the company you're in?

Why is this important? Well, in order for the opposite sex to value us we must first value ourselves. I once had a friend of mine, Olivia, who was always apologising profusely for absolutely everything. I mean so much that it was pretty irritating. Almost every word that came out of her mouth would be some sort of apology muttered under her breath. One day I had to ask her over a glass of wine whether she actually realised how much she apologised. She had honestly never even thought about it and when she realised she just stared at me in disbelief and said ,'Oh god, sorry am I?'

Fail!

The problem is, this level of over apologising doesn't just impact your love life. Olivia was one of the brightest girls I knew but she was never getting the promotion she wanted at work and felt she deserved more. Her demeanour was constantly so apologetic that people didn't see the strength in her to give her the greater responsibility she craved.

To summarise, there's nothing wrong with being polite and apologising when it's necessary to, but really – try to save your apologies for moments that matter rather than throwing them away when you needn't.

According to Beverly Engel, author of _The Power of Apology_, very often, children who have been brought up learning to deal with a great deal of responsibility for any problems or issues that arise from a very young age are more likely to over apologise than those who weren't, as are those with parents who instil apologising as a form of politeness. This may go some way to explain why those public school boys and girls are perceived as ever apologetic. Many went to boarding schools where they had to not only behave in very polite manners, but they also had to take on responsibility at a young age by learning to live without their parents.

Don't compete with other women

Often, strong, articulate and confident women are very empowered in all aspects of their lives, except their relationships. They have wonderful jobs, great families and are proud of the achievements they have amassed to date. You put them in a boardroom, and they command a room. You put them in an office, and they are competitive and strive to reach the top ladder of their careers. You put them in a social scene, and they are the centre of attention and the life and soul of a party. Depending on their personality types, they thrive on the buzz and attention they derive from being powerful leaders.

Often, however, they fail to leave these traits 'at the office' so to speak, so when it comes to finding a chap they can often be very competitive with other women - similarly to how they might behave in a boardroom. Some women feel that eligible men are so few and far between that they must be ruthless in their pursuit of them and do whatever it takes to get their attention. Unfortunately, this can often be at the expense of their relationship and friendship with other women. I have personally seen first-hand situations where strong and confident women will purposefully interject a charming man having a conversation with another woman and place themselves in between the two of them in order to try to get his attention. Not only does this give you a bad reputation with men (as it really does look a bit desperate), but it certainly doesn't help you make friends with women either. I don't know about you but I'm a big believer of women looking out for and supporting each other as much as they can, not being jealous or competitive and fighting for attention.

I once had a client of mine, Henrietta, who lived in Chelsea, and she was a perfect example of how not to behave in this scenario. At age 47, she had been divorced for almost ten years and was starting to panic that she would never find the man for her. When she came to see me she was so confident, successful and attractive, I honestly thought it would be fairly easy to find her a nice match. Without batting an eyelid I therefore introduced her to several of my male members, one of whom she really took a liking to. They both fed back that the date had gone well, but Charles (the chap I introduced her to) was perhaps less glowing in his praise for how the evening went. He was not keen to go on a second date with Henrietta, and despite her disappointment she politely said she, of course, understood. The forces of fate being what they were, interestingly Henrietta went back to that same bar with some friends a couple of weeks later for a few drinks, and lo and behold in walks Charles with another woman, on what appeared to be a romantic date. What should have Henrietta done? The ideal scenario here would have been for Henrietta to leave them to it, not interrupt them and only upon leaving or directly crossing his path, politely say hello and that she hoped he was enjoying his evening – courteous conversation basically. Instead, what did Henrietta do? She walked directly over to Charles mid-conversation with his date, and told him she needed to talk to him, rudely pulling him away from the situation. Unfortunately, this only ended up embarrassing everyone involved. Charles felt awkward in front of his new date, and the lady he was with found it to be nothing but rude. Henrietta got

'When you are content to be simply yourself and don't compare or compete, everyone will respect you.' Lao Tzu

nothing out of it either as when she did pull him away for a 'chat', she really had very little to say to him. According to Charles, she just wanted to find out how he was. Essentially, what happened was that Henrietta was so used to being in control of all other aspects of her life that she found it incredibly difficult to just let go of someone she found attractive, especially considering she was starting to panic that the quality men were very few and far between. I'm afraid, ladies, that behaviour of this manner only reinforces to the chap why he wasn't interested in you in the first place. It also did nothing to help Henrietta's reputation as it turns out that the date he was on had several friends in high places, and word quickly got around that Henrietta was one to watch, and her social card was unfortunately well and truly marked.

Never compare yourself to other women, and if a man displays interest in someone else, let him. You simply can't be everyone's cup of tea and there's really no bigger turn off for a man than someone acting desperate to get attention or get noticed (unless they are a stripper or a pole dancer), so most of the time this is regarded as an enormous faux-pas. Remember, you're better than that and you certainly don't need to lower yourself to such demeaning behaviour.

Make Time

I can't tell you how many women I know genuinely think they're making an effort to find love while in reality they are putting in crazy hours at work or at the gym. I know life can often get in the way, and there will always be times when you have to put in overtime at the office at the expense of your social life, but don't let that become a comfortable excuse for why you haven't met someone nice. If you're a career-minded woman, good for you, but do try to make time or use what free time you have wisely to try to avoid having an uneven work/life balance. Don't make making time something you're going to regret doing in later years, do something about it now.

Also, if you're working so much that you seem to be mixing your work and social life, and find yourself doing work dinners or drinks several times a month with clients or colleagues, try to think about how much time you're really committing to yourself. Whilst you may use the excuse that it's work related and that you need to go for your job's sake, are you sure you really need to go to every thing? Don't hold yourself back by convincing yourself you are too busy when you could just be choosing to spend your time in different ways.

If you do schedule in some dates to your busy diary, however, be careful not to treat your dates like an interview or business meeting. The purpose of meeting someone new should be fun, not overly formal or process driven.

Let's Look At Him

How to get him interested

Get his interest immediately

It's often been said that, within the first 10 seconds of meeting someone, fundamental questions are asked and answered subconsciously in our minds before we determine whether we like them. We often don't even realise it, but each and every acquaintance we meet is put through this process of internal questioning. This is most likely to be especially the case in the UK, where we tend to be more reserved and rely more heavily on our perceptions than our communication. Therefore, really considering how you come across can be crucial to bear in mind when on the look-out to finding that someone special. Why? Because within the first ten seconds it can often be decided whether there is any form of attraction, and whether flirting can and should continue.

So what happens if you decide you quite like someone and think they are attractive? Interestingly, we'll take our theory of what we've gleaned in the first ten seconds and subconsciously try to prove that we are correct about that person, looking out for the signs that led us to believe a person is that way. For example, let's say you meet an alarmingly handsome guy at a bar who politely says hello and smiles at you. You immediately might think he's lovely and start looking for other qualities that qualify him as 'lovely'. On the other side of the coin, let's say your friend introduces you to a friend of hers but he abruptly says hello, avoids eye contact and seems disinterested. Your opinion of him will be that he's rude and arrogant, so from that point onwards, unless he does something remarkably charming, your opinion of him will be formed subconsciously as rude and arrogant.

So what should we be aware of if we are keen to give off the best impression of ourselves? What simple things can we do to ensure we're looking as approachable and interesting as possible to encourage men to come over and talk to us? Understanding how to make a killer first impression is crucial if you want to understand how to make a desirable impact.

Body Language:

So how does what you're doing with your body give off information about you to prospective men? You might not realise it, but how you carry yourself and your body language speaks volumes about how you feel inside. You might not have paid much attention to your body language, but the next time you're out with friends, mentally evaluate your natural position by paying special attention to the following:

*   If you're sitting down, look at your arms. If they're crossed, uncross them and make sure your legs aren't pointed away from what's going on in the room.

* If you're standing up, put your shoulders back and imagine balancing a book on your head. Give yourself poise and you will immediately seem more intriguing.
* Don't fiddle with your hair, face or jewellery as these are telltale self-comforting motions people do when they are uncomfortable.
* Don't grip your bag tightly for support or anything else nearby you can hold onto (including drinks; best not to knock them back with gusto).
* When talking to anyone, don't take yourself too seriously and laugh as often as you can. Make some funny comments and you'll be sure to lighten the tone and relax everyone around you too. Smile, it's contagious!
* When you're anxious, try to raise your voice slightly when talking to people. When you speak at a slightly louder volume, it subconsciously empowers you to feel bolder.
* Use mirroring if you're standing nearby to someone you're interested in. Follow his body language movements to signify that you share a common ground (more on this later).
* Don't keep looking around the room when you're with your friends, checking for who's there. A quick glance when you arrive is fine but if you're constantly looking around, rather than engaging in conversation, you'll only be giving off signals that you're insecure and uninteresting.

What's interesting is that when you adopt certain bodily stances you actually start to feel differently. If you stand taller with your shoulders back, for example, you'll actually start to feel more

'Good posture makes you look taller, slimmer, perter and more confident. Think tall, hold your head high, keep your back straight, shoulders back, tummy in and hips forward'
Debretts Etiquette for Girls

confident. The same can be said for smiling. You might not realise it, but smiling actually makes you feel happier. Even more reasons to smile as much as you can!

Whilst understanding your own body language is very important in order to give off the right signals, being able to read body language is also going to really work in your favour, as you can determine pretty quickly whether a guy is interested in *you*. Let's say you're out with some friends and you see a handsome chap at the bar. You haven't started chatting yet but you're keen to determine whether he's at all interested. Just watch out for some of the following clues that he might well be open to engaging in conversation:

*   Is he trying to look taller in your presence? Often men, when they see an attractive lady, try to stand taller and appear more strong and burly. Also, don't be surprised if you catch him holding his stomach in or taking off his jacket to let you see his manly physique!
*   Does he raise his eyebrows quickly when he first sees you? This is a real telltale sign that he's keen, as he's implying he's surprised and intrigued by your appearance.
*   Is he trying to attract your attention by standing in your line of sight? Often guys in Britain – rather than

approach ladies directly – will gravitate closer to something they like gradually. So if he's moving in your direction over the course of an evening, it's a good sign.

* Is he playing with his glass? Often, if a chap has had his interest piqued he will start playing with his drink. Why? Because you're reminding him of sexual thoughts! So if you catch him swirling the liquid around in his pint glass, this might well be because you are reminding him of something else.
* Is he doing self-comforting motions such as playing with his hair or touching his arms or chest? This means he's actually self-conscious about how he's coming across and through these motions he's actually trying to make himself more comfortable.

www.sovainbooks.co.uk/bodylanguage

Command a Room

A really powerful way to command attention in the right way is to know how to work and own a room. How often do you find yourself going out with some friends, only to meet up and head straight for the back of the bar? It doesn't exactly spell out confidence and eligibility, and unfortunately, if you don't give yourself enough time to own a room you might be missing what's inside it.

Make sure you always enter with a purpose and stand tall. Many women enter a room timidly because they are keen to try not to appear too arrogant, and whilst you don't want to be seen to be over the top about it, it doesn't hurt to enter a room with a bit of a spring in your step. One tip I always advise my clients is that whenever you're going out to meet anyone, you should stand at the entrance for several moments just looking around before moving anywhere. Not only does this let you scan out the atmosphere and identify your friends as well as new people you may potentially like to talk to, but it also let's other people see you. You might like to do a little wave to your friends at this point, before confidently walking over to them and kissing them hello on both cheeks.

Theodore Roosevelt had a famous reputation for knowing exactly how to command a room.

According to historian Edmund Morris, his assemblymen remember him entering office on his first day by bursting through the doors and then pausing for a few moments to let everyone absorb his presence. Apparently this became a lifelong habit of Roosevelt's and he would bound from room to room in the White House.

The Rise of Theodore Roosevelt

Don't sit straight away

You also need to be super mindful of where you're placed when you go out. If you head to a bar and decide to find a table and sit somewhere near the back where you can put your feet up and be comfortable – because let's face it, those heels are only comfortable for so long – then you might want to consider other shoes.

Being in an area where you can be approached, or better still where natural conversations can just happen, is key, and in Britain this is the good old 'bar' where, as I've mentioned before, is one of the very, very few places where it's socially acceptable to strike up a conversation.

If you go and find your comfy seat at a table, you are immediately limiting your chances – which are already slim in Britain in the first place – of meeting anyone interesting. Guys are very aware of this by the way. Have you ever noticed that they don't all rush to sit at tables when they arrive anywhere, as they know the fish swimming near the bar are easily caught, whereas having to get a rod ready and cast it to the outer tables takes consideration and planning, and they won't see the value in going out of their way unless they need to.

Besides, a truly confident 'eligible' woman does not need to hide away at the back. Regardless of whether you're an introvert or extrovert character, you are a quality catch and you should find yourself in the prime pitch of the bar along with your glamorous girlfriends.

Don't be 'unfashionably' late

This is an interesting one that may be surprising to some, but if you're heading out with a few friends for some drinks somewhere or to an event that has a specific start time (such as a sporting event or bar opening for example) try not to be *too* late. I know often women like to be seen to be 'fashionably late' and not turn up to things on time, as it's often terribly awkward to be the first one to attend a party. Whilst I would agree that nobody feels particularly comfortable having to make endless, non-essential small talk by turning up to something too early, it's also mindful to try not to be *too* late either. I have organised events for some of my clients to meet when the chaps have arrived on time (often popping in on their way home) only to have had to leave before the ladies have even got there. The women spent so long getting ready or trying not to appear too keen that they actually missed meeting the prospective chaps.

What's more if you're always unfashionably late to events or parties you might miss the chance to claim a good position near the bar and watch out for potential eligible candidates who may walk in! Whilst it's ok to be a little late, don't overdo it as you may be doing more harm than good.

How to get him to come over

Don't overestimate male confidence

Yes, I'm going to say it. I'm going to put this out there. British guys don't have an awful lot of confidence when it comes to approaching or asking you out, or dating in general for that matter.

I always find this one of life's perplexities because often men are what I might deem 'overconfident' in other ways. I mean, you put them in the office, they are the king of their team, they are leaders in their field, experts in their industries. You take them to a dinner party and they compare the sizes of their genitals with regards to who went where on holiday or which restaurants you simply *must* try. You let them play sport and they are competitive bloodhounds, surging for victory, adrenaline raging through their veins. You tell them they are good at DIY and they will go to B&Q and buy a toolbox full of useless tools they may only use to put up the annual Christmas tree, but they will forever be lauded a 'handyman'. You get my point... The British man is actually rather confident, competitive and masculine in many ways, but for some reason unbeknownst to the most of us, absolutely not in a romantic capacity. They invariably don't know what they are doing and, therefore, have very little confidence in doing it, unless of course they are introducing themselves after several rounds of 'Dutch Courage' (which is often the case).

What this means in Britain, more than anywhere else in the world, is that we as women have to be nice to them when they go out on a limb. This often surprises other countries when I tell them this. I once caught up with two glamorous Italian friends of mine when I visited them in Rome, and told them about the culture of dating in the UK and how the guys just have very little confidence when it comes to chatting us up. For them, it's hilarious that men could be shy. They laughed heartily as I told them about it, and I kid you not whilst I was in the midst of my story they literally batted away two potential male suitors from approaching their table, later telling them off for interrupting them in the middle of telling a story. Now it's my turn to laugh. How cultures differ.

In the UK we do have to play the slightly softer hand when men try to approach, and always be gracious, courteous and kind to them. Even if you're not interested physically, there's no harm in talking to another human being for a few minutes. Plus, you never know, he may have been contemplating coming to talk to you for ages and waiting for the right time to pluck up the courage. Besides, it happens so infrequently these days, we as women should be encouraging the guys who do approach us, not shooting them down.

Whilst men are traditionally the pursuers, it's typically thought the responsibility lay with them to have the confidence to approach, but it's also up to women in Britain to have the confidence to know how to handle an approach. Be kind, be gracious, be charming, be polite and seem interested, at least at first. If you are genuinely attracted to each other, you can tone down how nice you are later on to keep him interested, but don't overestimate his confidence in the beginning. The fundamental reason for this is that, unfortunately, British men are culturally ill equipped to deal with emotions or feelings, and a lot of the time they are brought up believing that is what romance involves. It means you have to get all personal and mushy and stuff (uh, no thank you), so instead they choose not to approach women at all. Additionally, as I mentioned before, the more a chap actually likes you and finds you attractive, the less likely he is to come over and say hello.

The problem is that the girl assumes that because the guy hasn't come over he can't be that interested, and so subconsciously writes him off. I once had a really similar situation when I was single and a gorgeous guy had been giving me the eye all night only to finally pluck up the courage to say something just as I was about to leave (because I happened to need to get my coat from nearby his table). It was a shame as, had he made the move sooner, we could have spent the evening getting to know each other – but he lost out as I had to leave.

We as women, though, can adopt a few key tricks of the trade to encourage a guy to come over.

Don't go out with groups bigger than three

I know a lot of women feel more confident and popular planning evenings out with lots of people. The more the merrier. Besides, you're not going to say no to someone tagging along because it might ruin your chances of meeting someone of course. And absolutely, your life should go ahead as you deem it fit with as many people joining you on your evenings out as you like. You may just want to consider though that often for a chap (especially a chap who we already know is not as confident as we may like) approaching one girl is tough, approaching a group of girls is practically suicide. It's like a kamikaze pilot flying into what can only be perceived as a lose-lose situation.

So what you do if you're out with a group?

Split up. Don't spend your entire evening having group conversations but start chatting to one of the members and suggest you go get a drink by the bar. Find ways to break out of your group as often as you can. Make sure you pop to the loo frequently and check the room for any potential candidates, and when you come back to your group, position yourself in his line of sight so you can perfect your eye-contact skills.

Stop being shy and mysterious

I can assure you this really rarely works with British guys. Let's imagine you are out with friends in a nice bar or pub having a glass of wine and in walks a handsome chap who seems interesting. You can't quite work out whether you like him, but he's definitely commanded your attention. You look at him briefly and then look away focusing on your drinks and chatting to your friends. You have not smiled at him or looked at him for long, but somewhere in your mind you think that he will notice you and something will happen if he is interested; otherwise you're just going to dismiss him as being another guy who obviously can't be interested enough to bother to chat you up or do anything about it.

So far your tactics have been 'I'll be shy and mysterious, I have given him a quick look so if he likes me back he'll do something.' What I always struggle with is exactly what we are expecting the poor chap to do at this point? Do we expect him to stop what he is doing, and immediately strive forth into our lives, a rose between his teeth, and proclaim how beautiful we are? Do we assume he will come over and offer to buy us a drink as soon as he gets there? Do we hope he'll keep looking at us all night long and we'll play a game of flirtation stalemate? We honestly rarely know the answer because we rarely give enough signals to men to do anything about it.

As women, one of the key ways we can embody eligibility is to be confident enough to look at a man for several seconds and be gracious enough to do something very simple. **Smile**. Now I don't mean a weird, creepy smile that makes you look like you've been carefully watching him for hours, and I certainly don't mean just staring intently without smiling. The easier you find it to look at a guy and smile, the easier it will be for them to talk to you as you'll be giving off vibes that you are relaxed, easy going and approachable. Unfortunately though, what we often do in Britain is, if we see a handsome man, we look his way very quickly and then try to avoid further eye contact as we don't have the confidence to hold his gaze . By doing this however, you're simply not encouraging him enough, and, therefore, how on earth is he supposed to know that you are interested? Brits more than any other nation I know need more gentle encouragement before they approach a lady. They need to know they are safe and have very little chance of rejection before approaching a girl, so they won't be publicly humiliated. Try to be as friendly and open as you can from the moment you see a nice chap, so to encourage him to come and talk to you. If you do nothing and avoid looking at him, then don't be surprised if absolutely nothing happens as a result.

If you find this difficult at first, practice with people you meet every day. The next time you to go to work make a concerted effort to smile at people you meet on the train, or make eye contact with strangers when you're in line for your morning coffee. The more comfortable you are practicing on people you don't know and are not particularly interested in, the easier it will be when you meet a guy who has sparked your interest.

Building Rapport and Brilliant Banter

So you've got him interested by being your alluring and charming self, and you've encouraged him enough that he's now trying to initiate some sort of conversation with you. That's great! So now

> 'Rapport is the ability to enter someone else's world, to make him feel that you understand him, that you have a strong common bond.'
> Motivational speaker Tony Robbins

what do you do? Let's look at great ways to build killer rapport, get conversation flowing in a non-awkward manner and master the art of what we lovingly call good old 'British Banter'.

Do I like you? The rules of 'rapport'

We all like to be liked and creating a good rapport is a skill that everybody can develop and improve, and it's a really valuable to hone when it comes to dating. Some people are naturally blessed with the ability to build great rapport effortlessly. You probably know a few characters like this – they just have that natural charisma, that suave ability to make you like them pretty much instantly. They are disarmingly charming and instinctively you just trust them and enjoy conversation with them. But in reality anybody can learn the tools needed to build fabulous rapport, if they are willing to try.

Most of the time, however, us as Brits like to settle for the basic necessities of being nice. The must-do basics of being polite. Often anybody who's seen to go over and above the socially accepttable 'niceties' of conversation is often seen as trying too hard or a bit disingenuous. So how does one build rapport without being deemed as a bit of a crawler?

Let him dominate for a while

Human beings, like many animals in the animal kingdom that are programmed to respond to leadership and dominance, when we meet each other we might not realise it, but within the first ten seconds we tend to size each other up to decide who is the dominating figure. Most of the time this happens between the same sex, where men will try to outdo other men to claim their 'alpha' status or women will dress 'to impress other women'. It does also happen a great deal between men and women too and is firmly entrenched within the flirtation process.

Typically, as men are the stronger sex physically, they have traditionally assumed the dominant role and many years ago, when they were cavemen, this would have been in the form of bringing you food, providing you with shelter or fighting to prove masculinity. Today dominance can be seen in several ways, such as confidence, behaviour, social status, wealth and body language. I always find a good example of this can be found in any London nightclub when as soon as you walk in you see tables full of drinks such as vodka bottles, mixers and champagne. Usually it's a few flashy guys who have bought the tables and they invite attractive girls to join them. In this instance, they don't need to talk to prove their dominance (you often can't chat in these clubs anyway), as instead of saying it they are showing it, and the girls have picked up on that 'power' signal and respond by joining them for drinks.

The girls in response, who accept the invitation to their table, then seem to behave like they are prize possessions that are enjoying being treated. They coyly laugh at the jokes of their hosts, play with their hair and generally appear more submissive than they might normally behave.

Whilst men are typically more dominant, it certainly doesn't need to always be the case. Men tend to be more dominant as regards being competitive and aggressive, but studies have shown there is absolutely no difference between the sexes when it comes to leadership or assertiveness. Women can be equally as dominant if they are natural leaders and have an assertive air about them[2].

So what does all this mean when we first meet someone? Whilst I would never encourage or advocate any eligible ladies to ever change for a guy, you might want to consider changing for the first ten seconds. If a guy is trying to impress you, that's usually a sign he's trying to dominate the situation, so what you need to do is be gracious and let him. If after that he smiles or offers to buy you a drink, there's no harm in saying yes. Don't emasculate a guy by rejecting him or trying to be equally as dominant as him... at least for the first ten seconds!

Recognising how dominant you might be perceived is important if you wish to understand and control the signals you put out, but more importantly it helps you figure out what sort of character you're dealing with. If you can determine when he starts chatting to you whether he's a dominant character then you can choose whether you wish to adjust your behaviour accordingly.

Signs of power-play

* He may give you the 'big I am' and talk about how amazing he is. He may mention what he does for a living if he has a good job.
* He'll name drop places he's been to or people he knows into conversation.
* He might try to impress you with his wealth or intellect.

* Literally looking down on you whilst talking. Ensuring he's at a higher level than you physically, like sitting in a higher chair or standing whilst you're sitting.
* Speaking loudly or boldly, leaning back with open body language whilst doing so.
* Starting sentences with 'have you ever heard of'.
* Initiating or controlling the flow of conversation.
* Disagreeing with you and suggesting his own opinion.
* If he offers to buy you a drink, he might suggest what drink you might like (which, unless the drink sounds delicious, I hope all ladies would politely decline as it's very important to have your own opinion).

Signs of submissive behaviour

* Bad posture.
* Slumped or closed body language.
* A nervous and apologetic smile or laugh.
* Saying things like 'wow you're a bit out of my league'.
* Soft voice. You may often find yourself asking him to repeat what he said as you just can't hear him.
* Blushing when speaking.
* Shyness and social anxiety.
* Agreeing with things or failing to have his own opinion.
* Does what he's told.
* Cares what people think of him and may come across insecure.

Now, whilst these lists are reflective of what to be aware of from any potential love interest when they start chatting to you, you too may have a combination of these characteristics. Have you ever noticed how you're louder or quieter around certain people? Perhaps you're really confident among your friends but when you get to work you can clam up and tend to be a little more reserved? It's the same with people you could be attracted to. You'll decide within the first 10 seconds how you are going to behave by judging the level of dominance you exert or defer over the situation.

So just be aware of it, remember to embody eligibility and be confident, but it doesn't hurt to give the alpha male the satisfaction of leadership for the first ten seconds, if an alpha male is what you're looking for, of course.

Use mirroring

Another great tip to build rapport with someone you like is to mirror their behaviour and body language so you can reflect the person you're talking to. This is a great tool to help build mutual understanding and to say without using words that you like each other, that you agree, and that you feel the same. Essentially, if you mirror them, it's much more likely they will like and trust you and feel a certain connection to you – without necessarily understanding why, as most of this happens subconsciously between the parties involved.

Next time you start chatting to a new guy, make note of his posture, his gestures, how he's standing or sitting, what he says and the pace at which he says it. If you are on the same wavelength, you might mirror each other so much that you start to finish each other's sentences, and guess what he's about to say next.

Avoid mundane conversation

I'm not going to lie, sometimes conversation in Britain can be painfully awkward and mind-numbingly dull. We as a nation do love a bit of small talk and very few conversations go by without discussing the weather, or asking questions such as 'what do you do' or 'where do you live'.

Should you get to the point when a guy is chatting to you, what you want to do is avoid this awkward tension as quickly as possible and break the British ice, so to speak. Some fantastic ways to do this are by challenging the typical conversations conventions we are so used to as a nation.

So what is a typical conversation very often like for us Brits? Take a look at the following dialogue, which could be representative of chatting to any new person you meet in the UK, whether out and about socially or at work. We've all been there. Does any of it sound familiar?

> Him: Hi, I'm James
>
> Her: Hi James. I'm Alison, it's lovely to meet you
>
> Him: It's so cold today isn't it. I can't believe how much the weather has changed. It looks like it's going to rain later... again
>
> Her: Yes I know I'm having to wear several layers these days. It's so hard to know what to wear.
>
> Him: Yes I know, me too. So Alison what do you do?
>
> Her: I work in management consultancy for Bain
>
> Him: Oh right, I used to know a few guys who worked there. Have you been working there long?

> Her: Yes, about 10 years now, before that I was in finance. What about you?
> Him: I'm a criminal lawyer. Love to put the world to rights.
> Her: Oh wow that sounds interesting
> Him: So do you live around here?
> Her: Yes I live not too far away, by Wimbledon Common...
> Him: Ah right yes you're close to me, I'm not far from there. I'm based in Battersea.

And the conversation goes on in the same mundane way it started...

Now, the problem with this type of conversation is that whilst it's terribly polite, it's also incredibly boring and inevitably once it's over both parties will feel they have exhausted conversation for now and will not revert back to each other again. You often see this at cocktail receptions, for example. You've said hello to a person already, but because it was so mundane you really don't want to re-engage with that person. That's when you see people pretend they haven't seen each other or dart in other directions with haste – all very odd behaviour.

Most of the time what we tend to do is try to get through conversations without feeling like it was just one big awkward moment in our lives. Very rarely however, do we realise that we shouldn't just be trying to 'tolerate' conversations, we should be trying to make them great.

If you meet someone, whether it be someone you're romantically interested in or not, try to avoid mundane conversation as much as you can. If you do, you'll be deemed as far more interesting and refreshing, and you will probably make quite an impression. Here are some common British conversation starters that really are worth avoiding if you don't want to be faced with seriously 'awkward' chat.

Things you should avoid asking:

What do you do?

We as Brits love to talk about our jobs and what we do for a living. Whilst it's fair enough that you're showing an interest in the other person, this question is extremely loaded. The reason for this is that it can often seem like you're super keen to find out how much money they make, and from then make a judgement about them. This is not what you want when trying to make a good impression on the opposite sex, as he may think you're money-oriented. It also implicitly implies that you are associating who they are with their choice of career, when I'm sure most of us would agree that what we do has very little to do with who we are as a person, with our own personal goals and objectives.

Whilst you may be genuinely interested to find out what they do, asking this question too early can often be deemed rude and pretty much be a conversation killer – so it's best avoided at least until you have developed enough rapport with someone later down the line. Instead, it's far better to lead with topics that help keep the conversation flowing and that enable people to tell stories, rather than give one-word answers.

Talking about the weather

Yes, OK, the weather is often pretty bad in Britain. I admit it, I hate rain and I always say if I could pick up London with my hands and move it to sunnier climes it would be the most amazing city in the world. However, what we tend to do in Britain is use our shared hatred of the weather to form common bonds. It's something we all share so we feel we can all connect on the basis of talking about it. Many people feel that talking about the weather is what makes us so uniquely British, and whilst this may be so, I more often than not feel that anyone who brings it up is not looking for a meaningful conversation.

When chatting to a potential love interest then, if you start talking about or reciprocating on discussions about the weather, what you are basically saying is that you can't be bothered enough to make this conversation very good. What's more, most of the time when the subject of weather has been exhausted, there's often just an awkward silence while both parties start scratching their head trying to think of what to say next.

Yes I'm afraid to say weather chat does not a good conversation make however, so please avoid bringing it up if you can.

Where do you live?
If you think about it, why do we ask this question? Is it to find out if that person lives near to us so we can determine whether we have anything in common? Well, to a degree yes, that is true, but unfortunately also this one is a loaded question. A big reason why a lot of people ask the question (and both men and women are equally guilty of this) is because where you live can often say something about you as a person. It can quite quickly let people know what you are able to afford and therefore carries many associations along with it. However, when you're getting the ball rolling and making conversation with a new

chap, let him be interested in who you are as a person, not what your address says about you.

Get Better at Banter

The whole dating landscape can inevitably put a huge amount of pressure on us to find a date and feel attractive, but it's hugely important that you don't take yourself too seriously in the process. Brits love 'banter', so the less seriously you take yourself, the more people will warm to you and find you easy to talk to. It's all part of the self-deprecating charm! The less you worry about what you say and what others think of you, the more you will be able to focus on enjoying yourself.

Getting better at banter (or 'bants', as it's more commonly referred to these days) is therefore very important in British society and increasingly important when it comes to mastering British dating. In fact, one of the most common things I hear when getting feedback on dates is how good the banter was or wasn't. So much so, that more often than not is the term used to imply that the chemistry was or wasn't there, so it's so important that it's not overlooked. Often they'll say 'really funny girl, she had amazing banter and we just kept talking for ages', or I'll hear the opposite 'yeah really good looking guy, but the banter was non-existent'. If you're not analysing your banterful abilities, I strongly urge you to start.

But what is banter exactly and how do we get good at it? How does one perfect the playful art of witty conversation without coming across like you're just a bit odd? According to the *Oxford English Dictionary*, 'Banter' is defined as *'the playful and friendly exchange of teasing remarks'*. It's very popular in Britain because it's self-effacing; it's a way to poke fun of oneself, to appear humble whilst having a witty and dry sense of humour. Banter is also a cheeky way to disguise one's true feelings and defuse awkward conversations, which is another reason why it's so popular in Britain. If someone were to ask you a question you might not like, you can get out of it with a witty response. If there's a really awkward silence in the room and nobody is talking on a date, banter can often save the day. If you want to start having great conversations with practically anyone in Britain, it helps to have a bit of banter up your sleeve.

I think it's fair to say that, traditionally, banter was often regarded as something mastered and practiced by more men than women. They often partake in banter amongst themselves, mocking each other lovingly, and the man who can banter back the best is often the most appreciated in his group. A lot of the time too, women tend to want a funny guy, and I often find 'sense of humour' comes high up the charts in terms of what lovely ladies are looking for. Men, therefore, take pride in crafting their sense of humour. However, what women don't often consider is that the guy with good banter and a brilliant sense of humour also wants you to 'get the joke'. So if you don't respond in the light-hearted way he intended, he'll no doubt find you a bit boring and, I'll be honest, a tad slow. This applies not just to banter in person, but should you have any text or email correspondence before meeting you must ensure you apply a light-hearted lens to that too.

But there's a very thin line between banter and annoying sarcasm, so you've got to make sure you approach it the right way. If it's not coming across that you're one hundred per cent playful and joking you could be regarded as cynical and pessimistic.

* Make sure the person knows that nothing you're saying is serious. This is important; otherwise, this whole situation might become a bit awkward, so ensure you've built up enough rapport and that your body language is open and friendly. Remember to smile and make clear that you're enjoying the interaction with a cheeky glint in your eye.

* Be prepared to think on your feet when it comes to banter. It's a bit like improvised comedy. There are no rules per se, but you've got to understand the push and pull dynamics involved and be ready to respond quickly. Think fast and have quick wit.

* Don't leave it to the men to be the ones with banter. You can be funny and quick too! Just try to relax and let yourself enjoy the company you're in.

* If you're trying to establish banter via text or email, don't read too much into the messages you receive and be sure to respond quickly. So many relationships fail to take off because messages are overanalysed and they lose their comedic charm in the process.

* A little sarcasm is OK but don't be too sarcastic too soon. If you have literally just met someone and you start being sarcastic before forming any sort of rapport, you may just come across in the opposite way to how you intend to. Show your interesting side first and let your banter shine through afterwards. Also, if you're too sarcastic and cynical people will only think

you're trying to hide your true self and that you're not genuine.

* A really good way to get the banter ball rolling is to tease by saying something really nice and make them feel good about themselves, but then throw a slight cheeky insult in there somewhere. This is what's called 'push and pull' flirting. Whilst banter isn't prescriptive and there's no list of great banterful phrases to use (it really has to be interactive and free-flowing), bear in mind that you can be a bit insulting with a smile on your face and it can be very endearing.

Here is an example of how a dry, terribly awkward conversation with no banter might pan out, followed by an example of brilliant banter!

A Boring, Awkward Conversation

Him: Hello, I'm Toby, what's your name?

Her: Hi Toby, I'm Ophelia.

Him: What do you do Ophelia, are you from around here?

(She secretly wants to kill herself already for the mundane and incredibly dull question.)

Her: Yes, I live nearby, I'm an artist.

Him: Oh wow, does that mean you make stuff with your hands?

(she dies a little more inside)

Her: I paint with my hands yes...

(awkward silence)

She walks off, slightly disturbed and says nothing as she leaves.

A Banterful Conversation

Him: Hi, I'm Toby.

Her: Hi Toby, I'm Ophelia.

Him: Oh my God! You're literally the fourth Ophelia I've met today!

Her: Really? That's weird-

Him: No, in fact I've never met an Ophelia in my life, but I'm glad I have now as you are very lovely.

So, Ophelia, what brings you to this fine establishment?

Her: I'm an artist, this pub is right around the corner from my gallery.

Him: Oh my God this is awkward, are you going to ask to me to be your life model?

(She laughs)

Her: I usually wait until I've had at least two drinks down me before I ask men to de-robe themselves!

Him: Because I do have an exceptional physique, as I'm sure you can tell, so I'd be flattered if you did...

Her: Questionable shoes though, my brother had a pair like that when he was ten!

Him: Your brother must have been a very charming, witty and handsome child with exceptional style. So, Ophelia, may I buy you a drink?

Her: You may, but please don't feel obliged to de-robe straight away, you can at least finish your drink before you do.

Witty responses to dull questions

So, now you've got the idea and have a sense of what conversation with great banter involves, how do you apply it in practice? One of the easiest ways to ensure banter is to inject it into the conversation from as early as possible and to challenge mundane conversation openers right from the start. We already know we should seek to avoid bringing up loaded, dull questions such as 'What do you do?' or 'Where do you live?' but what should we try to respond to people who ask *us* these questions?

Here's a list of some commonly aske d conversation openers and some ideas for how to shift conversation away from the dull into the delightful.

How are you?

Boring Conversation	Banterful Conversation
You: I'm really well thanks, how are you? Him: Yes, not too bad thanks. *(Awkward silence as both parties think of what to say next and are bored already)*	You: You know what, I'm bloody brilliant. How could you tell? Him: I just had a strange feeling. I have a knack for these things. *(Both parties laugh a little and relax into further conversation)*

Do you live around here?

Boring Conversation	Banterful Conversation
You: Yeah I live not too far away so this is one of my locals. What about you? Him: Yeah I live up the road… *(Awkward conversation ensues due to the loaded question)*	You: Oh, God it's you again! I have told you to stop following me (with a smile) Him: (he laughs) Sorry I can't keep away obviously *(This gives you a great opportunity to divert talking about where you live too early on)*

Do I know you? You look familiar?

Boring Conversation	Banterful Conversation
You: Umm I don't think so. You don't look familiar. Him: Oh right, sorry. I must have confused you with someone else. *(Both parties awkwardly then try to avoid each other as they have run out of natural conversation)*	You: How could you forget a face like this? We've met loads of times! (Pause and look disappointed.) Just kidding I've never seen you before in my life. Him: (he laughs) Well that's a relief, that could have been awkward! *(You make the question seem less contrived this way as immediately you inject some laughter into the situation)*

So what do you do?

Boring Conversation	Banterful Conversation
You: I work in marketing Him: Oh right, which company? *(Conversation is then already going down a really dull route)*	You: What do I not do? Do you know I saved a swan crossing the road today? Him: Really? Where? *(This lets you deflect from the mundane question and guide things into lighter ground)*

www.sovainbooks.co.uk/banter

If he doesn't approach you

Now, I fully recognise that in Britain, even though we try to encourage men, often they will simply not come over. This could be because it's simply not convenient to them or because they want to save face in front of their friends. You might be out for dinner with a large group and he's there on a work jolly. Of course, one cannot guarantee that a chap will approach you, but there are a few cheeky things you can do to make sure you let him find you *afterwards*.

Many British men adopt the 'I'll contact her later' approach. Many more than you think, in fact. It's much easier to send someone an email or text after they have left and in this way avoid the face-to-face approach. Therefore, we as women need to play the game too and make sure we're leaving them as many clues as we can as to who you are so they can try to find you.

Get clever with business cards

In my opinion, there is nothing more awkward than someone getting out their phone and trying to sheepishly tap in someone else's number. Everyone is watching, all eyes are on the people involved and question marks are raised by witnesses over the reason for the exchange. It's nobody's business, but people will still judge it. Anywhere else in the world this is probably a totally normal exchange, but us Brits still find it slightly more awkward – as we do many things, it seems.

There is nothing more sophisticated, however, than the clever use of a business card. Clever does not mean handing them out like pamphlets to everyone you meet, but it means being very strategic about who you hand your card to, and how you do it. In fact, sometimes men can be rather good at this, slyly handing you theirs as a signal they are interested in you. If you're out amongst friends and two interested parties haven't had the chance to chat one-on-one but there was definite chemistry, often the guy will slip the girl a business card and hope she'll deem the fact he's given his card as 'an approach'.

But often women won't like it as it means they will have to initiate contact, which means the whole relationship will be off-kilter forever, right? The relationship will be doomed before it's even begun, and does this count as 'an approach' or is it a bit of a cop out anyway?

Normally I would agree, and say that in most countries if a guy hands you his card, it's probably because he isn't interested enough to put the effort in and wants you to do the legwork and call him. That's why the majority of relationship advice books you may read in your life will often say the same thing – that the woman should NEVER initiate contact if a guy drops you his business card. This is because in *most* countries, it's normal for a guy to approach and chase a woman.

In Britain, however, this is not the case, because a guy handing you a business card is essentially saying 'I couldn't get you on your own to ask you for your number and didn't want to embarrass us both by asking for it in front of loads of people, so please take my card and contact me instead, otherwise I'm worried I might not know how to see you again.' It's not because they are lazy and want you to do the work; quite the opposite, in fact. It's because they haven't been able to approach you in a non-embarrassing way so he's trying to ensure he doesn't lose contact with you. When women ask me sometimes whether they should ever contact a guy who slipped their business card, I will ALWAYS say, 'absolutely yes', because otherwise you might be missing a great opportunity.

However, bear in mind that in order for your response to be effective, it must be done with a certain amount of flair so he still gets the message that he has to put the work in to get you. When you message him you have to be so incredibly confident and charming, yet immediately put the ball back in his court. Here is a good example of what you could say.

> This business card appears to have been misplaced as I found it in my handbag this morning. Goodness knows how it got there. I don't mind looking after it for you, but feel free to give me a buzz on xxxx to reclaim ;-)

This sort of cheeky, confident message implies that you have a sense of humour, you're not taking the whole thing too seriously and you're immediately putting the ball back in his court to contact you.

Mention your full name

However, if you're still really not comfortable contacting the guy first at all, and that's fine as plenty of us would simply rather not, there are two options. The first option is that you get super confident with handing out business cards yourself and the second is that you learn to drop your full name into conversation, so that you can be easily googled or found on Facebook!

Now, even if you don't have a super high powered job or you don't work full-time, it doesn't matter. Get some business cards printed if you're single and start treating your single life like a really valuable networking opportunity. You don't have to hand them around to every Tom, Dick and Harry, but you can certainly use them when chatting to people as a way to let them know they can reach you. The beauty of the business card is also that it nicely masks the awkwardness of the romantic approach through a work disguise, even if it's not work related in the slightest.

A really good way to use your business cards is to be incredibly elegant and confident about the way you hand them out. If you find yourself truly stuck in a work-related conversation, as mundane as they can be (and ideally avoided as much as possible), you may as well make the tedious chat into an opportunity, especially if you find them attractive. For example, say you find out he works in corporate finance (or anything equally as obscure) you could casually drop in the following to the conversation:

> Him: Yeah, I work in corporate finance for a big multinational.
> (You try not to yawn)
> You: Oh really? That's interesting. I was just talking to one of my cousins who also works in
> corporate finance. He's just lost his job unfortunately; I can't remember the name of the company...
> Him: Oh gosh that's a shame, there are loads. Perhaps it was PWC, Accenture...?
> You: It might have been Accenture actually. Yeah really bright guy actually, but just starting out so I'm sure he'll find something soon.
> Him: Yeah I 'm sure he will!

You: Perhaps I can give you my card in case you guys know of anything, you can give me a buzz?
Him: Yeah absolutely, if I hear of anything I'll let you know.

The other option if you don't like business cards is to try to get used to people knowing your full name. A friend of mine, Joanna, had a great experience with this after she met a rather dashing chap at a work networking event. She didn't get the opportunity to leave her card but she did manage to drop in her full name. Now most people would assume you would forget someone's full name, but I assure you, if a guy is interested in you, he will be listening attentively. This guy was clever enough to Google Joanna's full name, find out the company she worked for and then work out the email address by the structure of the other email addresses on the company's website. They ended up having a few emails back and forth and are now happily married – and all because she happened to cunningly drop her full name into conversation.

However, leaving your full name need not apply to just work-related scenarios. The amount of people I know who have met and started dating via Facebook is also quite remarkable. If you're out with friends and there's a guy in the group who's interesting, he may well message you on Facebook if he works out your full name (or if you have any mutual friends), so be sure to try and drop it into the conversation at some point so you are leaving yourself open to be found online.

The DOs and DON'Ts of 'Early Dates'

Dating Etiquette

Fantastic! So, however you've managed it, he's asked you out. He's found a way to reach you and let you know he's interested in the most minimally cringe-worthy way possible. You equally have agreed in a minimally desperate way to go out somewhere with him. You're both well on your way to going on a typically British date, well done!

Now, you may notice that I have said *he* has asked *you* out, and not the other way around. This is not by accident and that's because whilst I am a firm believer that we should encourage the British man as much as possible to approach us and to talk to us in all the ways described up until now, I'm certainly not saying that we should be the one to initiate or lead the relationship from that point forth.

Call me old-fashioned, but when you've been gracious enough to encourage a chap to ask you out (and however it comes to fruition) he can take things from there. You're not there to hold his hand all the way. This is not me telling you to treat them mean to keep them keen, it is simply good manners on his part, as if a man wants something badly enough he will do something about it. Besides, if you are looking for a true gentleman then the very least he can do is be man enough to instigate proceedings by getting in touch with *you* and asking *you* out.

So how should we navigate our way to success through what I call the 'early dates'? These are the first couple of dates you will go on with a chap and are, in my opinion, the most crucial to get right should you be curious to take things further. It's during these dates that you work out whether you like each other, whether there's any spark and, should you get to date three, it's often a solid sign that things are going in the right direction. Getting through these 'early dates', however, can often be the trickiest part of any budding relationship, especially when dealing with British men who can often be quite non-communicative about how they feel and whether they like you. So what's the etiquette involved with who arranges these dates, where you should go, and what's the best way to keep a chap interested?

Who arranges logistics?

During the early dates, ideally, a gentleman would suggest a place to meet that he thinks you'll enjoy and that's conveniently located to you, and he will tell you when and where to be there. Don't fight it if this happens. Don't be difficult and try to move/change his booking if it's not your ideal choice of venue as it will only give off signals that you're high maintenance and difficult. At least wait until you've had a chance to get to know each other a little before you start making commands! The only time it's acceptable to niggle is if he's trying to get you to travel closer to him or put in any undue effort. This is a big no-no in the early stages, as the chap needs to be courteous enough to come to where is closer to you.

If you're not dealing with a guy who takes the lead in this manner (and many British men don't), then there are other things you can do. Perhaps your guy is a bit more of an introvert or a bit more indecisive, or perhaps in all fairness he simply doesn't know the area in which you live all that well to suggest where to meet. In this case, there is absolutely nothing wrong with giving him suggestions on where you could go. His fundamental goal should be to impress you so he will probably be grateful of any suggestion that limits his chances of getting it wrong. Do some research ahead of time and have a few great date options up your sleeve of places you've always wanted to try, so you can make life easier for yourselves. Keep on top of exhibitions or events you can go to in your area or new bars that may be worth a try. Just don't go overboard like a friend of mine did when she took making suggestions a step too far and asked a guy (ahead of their second date) whether he could get tickets to the Wimbledon quarter-finals. The guy she was dating didn't find it at all endearing and couldn't believe how cheeky she was to ask! It's fine to make suggestions, but it's best to keep them realistic.

If, however, at any point the guy likes your suggestions so much that he alludes to you making the booking or buying the tickets, be warned: he's not that keen and he's not looking for a serious relationship. I hate to break it to you, but if he's not making enough effort for your very first few dates, he never will. He has to be the one to make the necessary arrangements or else he's really not worth your time. You're better off waiting for a guy who values you enough to take the lead and the initiative.

What makes an acceptable 'early date'?

To dine or not to dine, that is the question. What makes a great first or second date? Is it better to just meet up casually for a few drinks or should a man be romantic enough to suggest a proper sit down evening meal right from the start? What other ideas for a date are acceptable when you're getting to know one another?

As we've discussed, us Brits hate awkward conversation and we prefer to acclimatise gradually to each other's company, so it's best to start with something short and sweet on your first date, and increase the amount of time you spend in each other's company gradually.

Therefore, what makes an acceptable first date VS a second date are two different things.

The first date is when you're not sure you're going to hit it off so it's best spent doing something where you can readily get in and out quickly if needs be. Therefore, in my humble opinion, dinner should best be avoided as there is nothing worse than feeling like you have to sit through an entire meal with someone you're not really connecting with. A dinner also denotes that you're free all evening, so it doesn't give you an easy excuse to duck out early should you feel you need to. Besides, you shouldn't really be looking to spend any longer than an hour and a half on your early dates (more on that later) as you do want to ensure you maintain a sense of intrigue and mystery.

Whilst a dinner should best be avoided on date one, there is nothing wrong however with eating *food* on a first date (and I would strongly suggest to actually eat food rather than play with it), so a spot of lunch, brunch or grabbing a coffee and cake are all absolutely fine, as these all take place earlier in the day and give you an opportunity to attend to the other items in your diary.

An acceptable first date is somewhere relaxed, informal and conducive to making conversation so as to give you both the opportunity to talk easily without interruption. It can certainly include a couple of drinks, but does not include getting so wasted that you forget the entire experience, or worst still – end up going home with him.

Acceptable First Dates:

* A drink at a bar convenient to you where you can relax and enjoy a couple of glasses of your tipple of preference.
* A quick coffee during the day is totally acceptable as it's very rare people drink more than one, so if you don't like each other it gives you an easy excuse to leave.
* Going for a walk around a park where you can get to know one another or visiting an exhibition or market nearby (so long as you have agreed this ahead of time so you are wearing the right shoes).
* A lunch or brunch during the day is fine as these can be informal and don't have to take too long.

Unacceptable First Dates:

* A formal dinner is too much too soon for a first date but very much welcomed further down the line once you have got to know each other. Save it for at least date number two or three.

* If a guy suggests a sporting event, it's not a good start. You need to spend quality time getting to know one another before doing the kinds of activities that involve you spending a significant part of the day together. It also implies it's something he likes and doesn't give the impression he's really thought of you and what you might be interested in.

* Meeting up at a nightclub after 11 p.m. does make a first date! Many British guys try this approach if you're out with your friends one night and so is he. He might suggest keeping in touch as the night progresses and may text you near to the closing time to suggest you join them. If this does happen, feel free to politely refuse. It's much better to wait for him to make the effort, and if he doesn't make the effort I'm afraid he's not worth your time.

* A date that involves dancing lessons. We're British, the majority of us have two left feet (myself included), so any date that involves a significant amount or rhythm is a big no-no until the ice has been firmly broken. Even if you're both amazing dancers, it's much better to opt for a date where you can both have a conversation.

* The cinema. Why would you want to sit there in silence with each other?

* A concert to go and see a band he likes. How does he know what kind of music you like? Besides, it's really difficult to strike up conversation next to a drum kit.

* Inviting your date to do anything that involves him meeting your friends is a bad idea. Not only can you

not really get to know each other properly, but it's just far too soon to be introducing him to anyone.
* Any date that involves you removing items of clothing is a big no-no. So no accepting offers to a spa day or pool party (not that we have many of those in this country).
* A date at his house. You don't know the guy yet so why would you go to his house? If he's suggesting it he's probably after one thing and one thing only. Ensure you go to public places until you feel comfortable enough around each other.

Once you've gone on a first date and it went well, you can then use your judgement to deem what kind of second date you feel comfortable going on. For some people it works to do something different (so if you met for a quick coffee on a first date, you might choose to meet for a drink on your second one), for others, a repeat of the first date is fine (so another drink somewhere else). If you do feel the first date went really well and he invites you for dinner on your second date, there's nothing wrong with that as long as you feel comfortable with that. Just be sure to try to keep it to no longer than an hour and a half and be the first to call it a night. If you're not sure you're quite 'there' in terms of dinner yet, then suggest something else that you feel more relaxed doing. Most importantly, just enjoy the process!

Which days of the week are good for early dates?

You might not realise it, but there is a certain unsaid rule in our great country that the weekend nights are off-limits until you get to know one another better. Friday or Saturday nights, therefore, are often considered somewhat sacred and saved only for the important people in your lives such as your friends, family and (because we are a nation of animal lovers) our dog. By either suggesting or accepting a date on one of those nights you might well be, without realising, implying one of the following things:

a. That you don't have a very good social life and have nothing else going on = sad and lonely.
b. That you are willing to give up your social life to find love = desperate.

Now this might sound ludicrous and you're quite right, it is. I'm sure in other countries it's not given a second thought, but in the UK us Brits find dating hard enough as it is without battling with the fear that we could be deemed lonely and desperate even before we have had the chance to properly meet up.

So should you wish to find yourself a nice chap, it's probably worth doing yourselves a favour and for the first couple of dates, even if they ask you in good time, say you are busy on a Friday or Saturday night. The best nights of the week for a first or second date therefore are either a Wednesday or a Thursday after work, and if that doesn't work logistically then a Saturday or Sunday afternoon will do just fine. All of these days are good options, as you will be more inclined to keep things short and sweet. If you meet during the week, you typically won't drink too much on what's considered a 'school night' and will have an excuse to pop off early for that 'early meeting at work' if you need to. Dating during the day, whilst often considered scary for many people, (as it somehow seems so much more formal and tense), is often better as you get to know each other without the Dutch (or British) courage we so readily depend on to unwind.

How much notice is acceptable before a date?

In Britain, because we tend not to give away our weekend nights to potential dates until we get to know each other better, we have a bit more flexibility about the days of the week that we choose to meet up. This means, therefore, that a few days' notice before a date usually suffice; otherwise, you run the risk of letting too much time go past without seeing each other and lose the momentum of interest.

Let's say a guy messages you on Sunday evening after you've met him out and about that weekend. He might ask to see when you're free and, depending on your diary, you might suggest Wednesday or Thursday. Both are absolutely fine. If you can't do either of those days, you would have to push the date back to a weekend day-date, or failing that it would have to fall into the following week.

You're much better placed not letting things drag into more than a week from when he initially suggested doing something; otherwise, he'll either think you're fobbing him off and aren't that keen, or you'll seem like too much hard work and he may lose interest. There are, of course, exceptions here and there, as there will always be things in your diary that you can't control. So should you have a busy period full of business trips or you're away on holiday, do let him know and apologise so he doesn't think you're blowing him out.

How long should you spend on a date?

When you're getting to know each other, it's crucial you maintain a sense of intrigue and mystery. Even if you have been introduced to your beau through mutual friends, have met online, or you've been friends yourselves for a while and have recently started dating, it's best to not give away too much romantically too soon. Ideally, therefore, for the first couple of times you meet up the whole thing should take no more than an hour, and at the very most (and only if things are going exceptionally well) an hour and a half. You should be aiming to gradually build up to spending more time together the more you like each other, so it's much better to start small and work your way up.

Why, I hear you ask, should you cut short what appears to a wonderful date? I mean, maybe you've both hit it off famously and you want to continue to enjoy each other's company. Neither of you are suggesting leaving so it's fine to stay and enjoy the time you have together, surely!

Well, ladies I'm afraid to say, and I'm going to be totally frank with you here – it's exactly the opposite. If you spend too long with a chap, several things will be happening to the dynamic of your relationship without you realising.

To explain, let me paint the scene. Let's say it's Thursday evening and you have a first date at a nice quiet bar near to where you live. He's arrived on time, you're five minutes fashionably late (no more as you're not rude). You immediately like each other, the ice has been broken by a witty comment he's made, and you're off. The date begins and it's going really well. You finish your first drink and he offers to buy you another and you think 'oh OK, yes why not', as there's no harm in having a couple of glasses. Besides, it's helping you relax. You both enjoy the second round, there's laughter, there's free-flowing conversation, there are flirtatious glances and there is chemistry in the air. You're having a great time and think to yourself 'I must have been here about an hour by now' but the date is going so well you're in no rush to leave. You have finished your drinks again and you're not sure whether he's keen to stay for another. There's a momentary silence in the room as you both try to determine what the other wants to do. At this point, what should you do?

a. You wait for him to suggest whether to have another drink or not and think, 'If he offers, he must be open to the idea — so I'll have one if he does'.

b. You notice his glass is empty and so is yours and say 'One more drink and we call it a night?' Besides, you're getting on so well.

c. You are the first to suggest calling it a night as you've had a couple already and feel that's enough for now.

What is the correct answer here? Yup, you guessed it – C.

You want to ensure you're the first person to suggest leaving for several reasons:

* You want to be giving off the impression that you are an eligible woman who has an awful lot going on in your

life and he's lucky to have had this time with you. You've got a busy day at work tomorrow and a jam-packed agenda.

* You want to maintain a sense of intrigue and mystery. Don't give away too much information about yourself too soon. Less really is more, so hold back on information and make him feel excited to get to know you better. If you have another drink he may find out more about you than you had intended to give away.

* You want to make sure the ball is in your court in terms of calling it a night first. You need to consider that if you don't do it first, then he might well do. This will only make you feel bad as you'll feel like he's got one up on you, and, unfortunately, he will probably pick up on the fact that you're more keen on him than he is on you. Not what you want.

I once set up a friend of mine, Sophie, with this really handsome army sergeant. She is an exceptionally attractive lady full of things to say, who had been single for a while after her ex unceremoniously dumped her due to commitment issues. Anyway, she's known amongst our group of friends for having a rather specific 'type' and being pretty fussy about who she dates so when she does find a guy she likes, she's guilty of being a bit over-keen. Sophie and this army sergeant decided to meet up for a day-date so went for a drink on a Saturday afternoon. It felt like a safe option as Sophie had plans to meet her girlfriends that evening so would have a good excuse to leave… or so she thought.

They got on so well that one drink turned into two, and two drinks turned into three, and three drinks turned into Sophie inviting this guy to come along and join her at the pub where she was meeting her friends. This handsome army sergeant agreed as he had some time to kill before he was due to meet his friends too, and off they toddled to the pub. What happened after the date was interesting though. Despite Sophie introducing this handsome army sergeant to her friends and them all having a wonderful time, it unfortunately took the power away from her as he was empowered to leave whenever it suited him. Whilst Sophie thought the date went really well, she actually never heard from the handsome man again. She simply gave away too much too soon about herself, her friends and her life and lost the intrigue she needed to keep him interested.

Who Pays?

This seems to be quite a contentious topic which causes much debate, as many people have different views of what is and isn't acceptable these days. Many people feel that because men and women are equal in so many ways, there should be some equality when it comes to paying for dates, especially as women can have higher salaries than men.

My view on this is very simple. If a man invites *you* out, then a good general rule is that he should pay for the privilege of your company, and seeing as he should be the one to invite you out during the early stages of dating he should pay for the first couple of dates. This is not because I don't believe in equality, I'm all for women and men being one hundred per cent equal in absolutely everything else in life, but just not when it comes to dating. It might sound old-fashioned to some readers, but I personally think it's just good manners. How can we expect to *find* a gentleman if we don't let men *be* gentlemen. We have to let them play the role of being masculine, being the protector, and being the provider at least for the early dates.

My other half often tells me that ever since we met he feels like he wants to be a better man (I know, he's very sweet), and that when we first started dating, because he was invested in the relationship, he actually enjoyed the process of organising and paying for the dates. When you find the guy right for you, he will *want* to pay and he will *want* to treat you and he will *want* to spoil you, not just because it impresses *you*, but because it makes him feel good about himself for being so chivalrous. So let him.

Therefore, my golden rule is that for the first two dates you should really let the chap pick up the bill. If a guy hasn't got as good a job as you have or you don't feel he can afford it, you shouldn't be made to feel guilty. He should only invite you to things he can afford to pick up the bill for in the early stages. You deserve to be treated and cherished so let him woo you!

Now, whilst you should always let a man actually pick up the bill (and hopefully he will want to) there is absolutely nothing wrong with making a subtle *gesture* to pay. This could mean saying something like 'Can I chip in at all' or reaching for your handbag. More often than not they will not let you but it can certainly go a long way to making you appear like you're gracious enough to offer. Some of my clients are the world's most successful men, but they still admit to liking it if a girl at least notions towards chipping in – even though they would never dream of letting her. You see, to a British man doing nothing when the bill arrives can actually be deemed to be quite rude as it makes them feel like you could potentially just be after their money or a free lunch, which as an eligible lady in your own right you're most certainly not. If they do accept your gesture of splitting it, at least on the first couple of dates, I would personally not be impressed in the slightest as it probably implies that the guy isn't that interested in you (or is just mean and stingy), as if he truly were, he would do whatever it takes to impress you.

If you're meeting for drinks and you order at the bar where there isn't a bill to split per se, then you shouldn't feel like you should do equal rounds. On the first couple of dates you should aim to have no more than a couple of drinks anyway (as you shouldn't stay too long), so don't feel like because he bought you one, you must repay the favour. You're not meeting a friend, this is a chap who needs to work to prove himself to you, the eligible lady. Further down the line, once you've become more comfortable with each other, you can judge how best to split things going forward based on the dynamic of your relationship. For some couples it works to split things 50/50, for others there's the one in three rule, whereby one in every three dates you have together will entail a small gesture on your part. I personally am a big fan of this concept and so would see no problem with you buying him a drink on your third date, or offering to cook him a meal at your home, so long as what you do for him is less grand than what he does for you. You don't want to emasculate him, and you want to make sure he feels and acts like a true gentleman around you.

Unfortunately though, I do understand that some men aren't quite as gentlemanly as they once were in this great country of ours, and often they don't like the sense that the lady is taking them for a ride. Whilst you should certainly be open to them treating you on the first couple of dates, don't use this as a weapon against them and try to get them to take you somewhere exceptionally expensive, unless, of course, they suggest it themselves. Also, don't expect or presume because they have treated you for the early dates that they will forever be your sponsor. Unless you happen to be dating an exceptionally generous man who strongly believes in playing the role of the provider, then it's probably best to be courteous and offer to pay on occasion.

Behaviour Etiquette

Now I'm sure that I certainly don't need to tell you ladies how to behave on dates. I have no doubt that most of you are quite capable of being your charming selves and getting through an evening with a chap you like quite effortlessly. The dating landscape is like a minefield, however, and there are inevitably things we can be aware of that might help smooth the process. Here are my top tips for certain things you might wish to consider.

Before a date: Things YOU should bear in mind:

Don't shout it at the hilltops

I know in Britain we don't get asked out very often and the prospect of a date can be as terrifying as it can be exciting, but do try not to announce it to all your girlfriends, colleagues, family and whoever else will listen. Whilst I'm sure they will be extremely happy for you, you really don't need the added pressure of having to tell them all the whole story if for some reason it doesn't work out or if you're not that keen. Save yourself the drama and don't mention it to anyone until you've met up and you feel there's a story to tell.

Stop yourself from being an online stalker

We as a nation love the Internet. We love browsing, shopping, researching, dating, playing and doing whatever else that takes our fancy online. The thing is, we have all become rather used to googling pretty much everything, including our potential partners. When it comes to dating, very often we get so nervous and inquisitive that we want to know everything about the person before we've even met them. We start looking for answers without knowing what the questions are and can find ourselves trying to look up whatever we can about the person online. If you know his full name, you therefore might start with a simple Google search, which might then bring up his Linkedin profile so you can see where he works. That might then lead you to have a quick check on Facebook to see whether you have any mutual friends or if you can see some more photos – and all of this so you can form an idea of what kind of character he is before you've gotten to know him properly. I must stress, if you are guilty of this behaviour (and I suspect many of us secretly are) you're much better off stopping yourself in the act as all this does is make you more anxious and facilitates you forming preconceptions about that person, which might be completely off the mark. Step away from the computer!

Also, it might sound like common sense, but if you have googled him, for goodness sake, don't let him know that you have. Don't bring up during your date that you found out he liked sports as you came across a JustGiving donation page for a charity marathon he ran three years ago. He'll only think you're a little bit strange.

It's a date, not a fashion show

Whilst it's understandable you want to look your best, just remember it's a date, not a fashion show. Try to avoid trying on outfit after outfit in front of the mirror before your date, as it will only make you feel more nervous. Remember, you are an elegant and eligible lady so he is the lucky one as he's getting the chance to meet up with you. Also, remember the cardinal rule about dressing elegant not sexy. Stick to a style that suits you, not what's currently in vogue.

Don't blow him out at the last minute

If you're not sure you're keen, perhaps you have an online date and you can't be bothered as you don't think he's your cup of tea, don't be rude and blow him out at the last minute. Should you wish to cancel your date, that's fine, but just be sure to do so at least 24 hours before so you don't come across as rude. You wouldn't like it if the shoe was on the other foot, would you?

Before a date: Things you should expect from HIM

He should be firming up plans

So, he's organised the date and you know where and when to be there, but if a guy is genuinely engaged with the concept of meeting up with you, it's courteous to get a text to firm up plans. Depending on when the actual date is planned, this text should either come through the day before or at the very latest the morning of the date itself. If a guy doesn't message you to firm up, he's playing it far too cool.

What you mustn't do is send him a message if you don't hear from him, asking him whether you're still on for the date. That just won't do you any favours and you'll sound a little too keen and dramatic, and it will make the guy feel a bit pressured. Instead, you can say something like 'Hi, just to let you know that I'm going to be running a few minutes late this evening. How does 7.15 work for you?' A message like that implies that you're still expecting to meet, but doesn't make you sound like you're disappointed to have not heard anything.

During a date: Things YOU should bear in mind:

Don't be so late that it's rude
I fully understand that a lady does not want to be seen to be the first to turn up to a date, and wait there for the guy. This only makes her look a little too keen. However, you also shouldn't be too late that it could be deemed rude. Five or ten minutes grace is absolutely acceptable, but don't push it or you could be giving off the wrong signals.

Give a really warm greeting
We as Brits can be a funny bunch. We no longer have a standardised way of saying hello to each other as the 'how do you do' has disappeared from modern dialogue. There's, therefore, no official greeting like the two or three kisses on the cheek that you see in other countries. Don't make the greeting awkward. Be warm and friendly and give the guy a

large smile, and if you feel comfortable enough go ahead and give him two kisses upon greeting. This will really help break the ice as you've already established some sort of contact.

Don't look bored

Could you imagine if you were talking and somebody just looked bored and uninterested the whole time, eyes darting around the room to check out everyone who walked in or everything else that was going on other than that person they are with? Even if you're not sure you click romantically, pay attention to who you're on a date with and try to feign interest in what they have to say. It's simply terribly impolite otherwise.

Laugh

Even if you don't find his jokes that funny, try your hardest to laugh and smile as much as you can in order to break the ice. Don't sit there and wait for him to amuse you, be open to enjoying yourself and he'll enjoy your company a whole lot more. Laughter can go a long way to making you both feel infinitely more relaxed. Just try not to giggle incessantly like a teenage girl!

Put your phone away

Yes, away. Don't put it on the table turned over, put it in your handbag. If for any reason it rings, it's really terribly ungracious to answer when in someone else's company. Put it on silent and apologise. Many of us Brits are simply slightly addicted to our phones. We rely on them for moral support so we can avoid looking at strangers. I often make note when I travel around

London quite how many people are either looking down at their phones for the sake of it (so just mindlessly checking a Facebook feed) or listening to music. Be confident enough to look up from your phone into the eyes, heart and mind of the person you're with.

EAT!

If you decide to go on a date that involves food (hopefully not dinner if a first date, as previously mentioned) then please try to order actual food and actually eat it. There is nothing more off-putting for a guy than a date with a girl who orders a lettuce leaf as she wants to give him the impression she's dainty and girlie. All you're really saying by not eating anything is that you're potentially pretty insecure as you don't feel comfortable enough eating a good meal in front of a guy, or that you're really high maintenance and fussy. Don't get things the wrong way around and think you'll be deemed more attractive to the guy if you don't eat anything. He's far more likely to be able to build rapport more easily if you have a good appetite. On the other hand, if you do order food, you might want to consider how easy it is to actually eat it without either getting it all over your outfit or your face. So if you're not proficient with twirling spaghetti, order the ravioli instead.

Don't drink like a fish

I know dates can be scary but don't try to loosen up by sipping on your drink repeatedly, and consequently drinking far too much. Remember, early dates should be short and sweet, so you should really only be able to have a couple of glasses. If you're past the early stages though and are having a meal together or a more notable evening then remember not to get too drunk, you'll only lose control of the evening and things could regrettably get out of hand.

Don't let someone off because you like them

If you're going on a date with a guy who seems like the most gorgeous man you've ever laid eyes on and you're really attracted to him, don't let him get away with bad behaviour. Some ladies can often turn a blind eye to things that, if done by anyone else, would only be deemed rude. If he's discourteous with the bar staff, or disrespectful of you in any way, don't take it. You are an eligible and attractive lady and don't need to be putting up with his silly antics.

During a date: Things YOU should expect from him:

He should get there early

It's common courtesy for a chap to realise that you might feel slightly embarrassed if you arrive at a date before him, so he should be aiming to get there five minutes early so as to be there when you arrive.

Greet you properly

You're not the only one to give a warm greeting. He too should greet you respectfully. If he's seated, he should stand up when you arrive, and if he's a gentleman, offer to take your coat.

He should not order for you

Many men think that taking the initiative when on a date impresses women. Therefore, occasionally you might encounter a chap who thinks he knows what it is you like and will endeavour to order it for you; whether it be a drink or food. Whilst this may impress some women, I'm sure it won't go down well with charming, elegant ladies such as yourselves, who have their thoughts and opinions. A true gentleman will not presume to know what it is you like without getting to know you properly first.

He will not comment on your choice of food or drink

I already mentioned this, but I want to repeat that, just because he doesn't want to order something, it doesn't give him the right to make rude remarks about your choice of food or beverage. Any man who says, 'God I don't know how you can eat that' is simply impolite. What you choose to order is your business and should not concern him, so should this happen, be gracious enough to smile and say something witty like, 'Yes I have a rather adventurous and developed palette, I love exciting things'. This will firmly put him in his place.

If it goes well he should make mention of seeing you again

If you are having a great time on your date, the chap should mention at some point before you say your goodbyes that he would like to see you again. If he's a gent, he won't leave you guessing that he's interested and will subtly suggest doing something again soon.

Great date conversation

We've talked about how to use great banter when flirting and when you want to break the ice, but how do you ensure the conversation during your dates flows easily and without awkward silences? Generally, the more you click with a person the less you will find yourselves running out of things to say, and the easier the whole experience will feel, however, there are certain things you can bear in mind that will take your dates to the next level.

Pay Attention

Sometimes women can feel terribly self-conscious when they go on dates. They might have checked themselves in the mirror several times before leaving the house, and when they arrive at their date they feel very self-aware – so much so that it's to the point of distraction. Don't get so caught up in yourself and think too much about what kind of impression you're giving out that you forget to listen to what your date is saying. Listen attentively to everything they say and try to really focus on them when you're with them. It doesn't give a very good impression if you get to date two and completely forget what you asked them on date one because you weren't listening. So, if he talks about his job or family, for example, make mental notes to remember the details.

Great conversation actually often involves learning to master the art of listening rather than talking. Let him finish his sentences before you interrupt and avoid turning things he says back to you. If he tells you a story, don't try to outshine it, but give a better example of something *you* encountered. It's not polite and won't do you any favours.

Also, don't ask a guy to repeat himself too much because you weren't listening. I have a friend who's really guilty of this. Whilst she's a lovely girl, her listening skills leave a lot to be desired and I'll often find myself noticing her eyes glaze over when you're in the middle of telling a story or explaining what you got up to at the weekend. The problem is, when you finish telling the story, she's the kind of girl who'll ask you questions and want details that you sort of already answered mid-story, it's just that she wasn't paying attention. If you're on a date, try to be on the ball and try to sharpen up as much as you can to really give the best impression of yourself.

Don't talk about yourself

A lot of the time women, unlike men, feel more relaxed when they talk. We are naturally more emotional and generally more communicative, so a lot of the time we like to get things off our chest. If you're on a date, as much as you might feel nervous, try not to get instances of being effusively chatty where you get into long reams of conversation about yourself. The British man is generally far too polite to pick you up on it and will probably just sit there and let you carry on, but he'll secretly be thinking 'get me out of here'. Make sure that the conversation doesn't remain solely about you and that he's the only one asking the questions. It's important to balance the scales, so if you find yourself going off on a bit of a monologue, take a deep breath with a smile and say, 'Anyway, enough about me…'

Ask open-ended questions

Whilst it's important to ensure you ask a lot of questions, make sure you carefully consider the type of questions you ask and how you ask them. Rather than asking him things that will inevitably result in a one or two-words answer, pick questions that enable him more opportunity to elaborate. Also, be careful not to line up question after question in a robotic manner. Wait for the guy to finish answering each one and space it out so it feels natural.

Some good examples of a few relaxed, open-ended questions could include things like: 'What did you get up to today', 'What do you normally like to drink?' or, 'How did you get into that job?' So instead of, 'What did you study at uni?' it could be, 'You studied Economics right?' Questions like these let the guy chat pretty informally without abrupt pauses. Whilst I'm sure I need not tell you ladies, it's best to avoid questions that seem somewhat overly scripted or insincere. Questions such as, 'What excites you?' or, 'What are you passionate about?' just sound a bit creepy and overly scripted. The idea is to let conversation flow effortlessly without feeling forced.

Compliment Him

It will unquestionably make for a more relaxed setting if you throw a little compliment into the mix to make him feel good about himself and give him a little ego boost. This doesn't mean you should dish out compliment after compliment, but one or two small and specific things can go a long way. For example, if you're meeting him at a bar that he has specifically picked out, it wouldn't hurt to say, 'This place is such a great suggestion, I love it!' or if he's wearing an unusual pair of shoes, mention how much you think they suit him. Also, it's worth bearing in mind how to compliment him to flatter masculine energy. So avoid saying things like, 'Oh you're so sweet!' or, 'Ahh bless!' as it will only insult his manly pride and make him feel slightly emasculated.

What to avoid talking about

I'm sure we all know the age-old rules about not to bring up religion or politics on a date. You never know what the other person's opinions are so it's best not to rock the boat too early on and leave such topics until you feel you know each other a little better. In addition to those though, if any of the following words are uttered by you or a date, you might like to swiftly reconsider what you're saying or change the subject immediately. These are guaranteed ways to either make the conversation awkward, or make you look like a show off:

'My ex was amazing'

Even if you both ended things really amicably and are 'still good friends', your date won't enjoy hearing about your 'him', as he'll probably think he's either still around, or that you're not completely over him. There's nothing wrong with telling your date how long you've been single if it comes up in conversation but don't ever mention how your last relationship ended, how he broke your heart by cheating on you or conversely how amazing he was and how you think you'll never meet anyone else like him.

'I made good money so...'

Talking about money is terribly un-British and very unnecessary when it comes to dating. Often people, especially in big cities such as London, have a tendency to value themselves based on how much money they make rather than what kind of person they are. Should the topic of money be raised on a date in any capacity, it's much better to change the subject onto more interesting matters. Besides, if he's a true gentleman, one would hope he would be humble and self-deprecating rather than flashy and ostentatious. The same can be said of an eligible lady, who would never be so rude as to be inquisitive about the amount of money a chap makes. Furthermore, if you are dating a chap who's recently gone through a divorce, you don't want to ask anything about the settlement or the child support (heaven forbid!).

'I love being kinky'

Any sexual opinions or preferences are certainly not appropriate topics of conversation for a date, and should a chap try to lead you down this path of conversation, do not entertain him. Unfortunately, whilst I believe every woman has a prince out there for her, she inevitably meets a few frogs along the way, and should you be unfortunate enough to meet a guy who asks you questions you're not comfortable answering, politely change the subject.

'I was so lazy, I only went to the gym four times this week'

Keeping fit is absolutely great and obviously really important to your general well-being. However, don't use a date as an opportunity to talk about how many classes you do each week and what your weekly routine consists of in detail. You should be going to the gym to look and feel good, not to talk about it incessantly. There's nothing wrong with mentioning you keep fit and enjoy going to the gym, but you might be best placed cutting out all the info on what your weekly fitness schedule consists of as you'll only come across as a bit of a show-off.

'Oh, my God, I have to show you this YouTube clip'

We, as a nation, love to laugh, and we often use humour as a way to bond with people, which is absolutely fine. The British dry sense of humour is as infamous as perhaps its fish and chips and I am a big fan of the infectious way we all respond to it. However, when on a date, please do not encourage or reciprocate anyone showing you a funny clip on YouTube or Facebook. Whilst this might be funny and acceptable with friends you know well, sitting there awkwardly watching a video clip on an iPhone is really not funny and is incredibly uncomfortable when on a date. Should a guy ask you whether you might have seen said clip, and you haven't, do not encourage him when he gestures to show you. Politely turn his attention to another matter and instead say, 'Don't worry, I think I'll look that up when I get home.'

'My day at work was hideous; I didn't stop all day'

It's really advisable to leave your work at the office if you can. Unless you have the most exciting job in the world, most jobs are pretty mundane and dull and generally people do not really enjoy talking about them. If you meet up with your date after a really busy day at work, and you haven't had a chance to stop all day, you don't have to share all the details with him. As much as they might politely listen, they're not going to care much for your stories about how badly your afternoon meeting went or how much you don't get on with your colleagues. A bit of information about your job is fine, but just avoid getting carried away.

'So my friend is friends with Kate Moss'

If you have famous friends, or friends in high places who might be well connected, it's really not advisable to start namedropping them on your dates as it will only make you appear as though you're a bit insecure. Interestingly, a lot of people think that mentioning that they are connected to someone of interest or 'power' makes them more interesting themselves. Unfortunately, talking about other people who you deem to be of interest on a date will not make you more interesting, only excruciatingly irritating and far more dull. Make sure you have enough good conversation up your sleeve to not need to try to impress through your connections.

'I had my appendix taken out, the bleeding was horrific'

Conversation can often feel awkward enough on a British date without making the other person feel even more uncomfortable by bringing up stories about a recent operation you might have had. If you've recently gone through some sort of surgery, then you'd be well placed to leave out the details of what it consisted of. What happens is, when you tell a story of yourself going through a bad time such as an injury or operation, your date gets a mental picture of you in that negative condition in his head. It's much better to give him positive associations of you in the early stages than letting him imagine you in a hospital gown feeling sorry for yourself.

To kiss or not to kiss

You've had a lovely time on your date, and when it's time to leave, you both walk gingerly out of the bar making the customary rumblings of how you are planning to get home, when suddenly, it hits you. You realise he might be about to make his move. You're not quite sure if he will, and as awkward as it feels to know that he might, you try to act nonchalantly and as though you are totally unaware of his thought process. Then suddenly out of the blue he leans in. What should you do?

If you like the guy then go for it, there's nothing wrong with a kiss on an early date as it lets you know he's interested and gives him a bit of motivation to see you again. If you're not sure, you'll know it, so don't try to over-analyse things too much. Just let the chemistry do its thing. If however, you find yourself in an awkward situation whereby he starts leaning in to make his move, don't do what they do in American movies and tell him that you're just not looking for anything right now and have a heart to heart with him about your feelings for him. There is nothing more awkward for a British man than blatant truthfulness. Just swerve his advances and give him a kiss on the cheek, then say your goodbyes. He will get the hint without anywhere near as much embarrassment!

Why you shouldn't invite him back

A kiss is fine, but if you're not both after one thing, do not invite him back nor accept an invitation to go back to his place during the early date phase. It's crucial that you resist the temptation to head straight to what you ideally need to be building up towards. A lot of women get insecure and worry that men won't like them enough to bother vying to see them repeatedly and will lose interest if they don't give them what they're looking for. It's actually quite the opposite, as men love the thrill of the chase and the mystery that surrounds you when you hold back from giving them everything at once. As soon as they have slept with you, they are far more likely to lose interest than they would have had you sustained the intrigue around you for much longer. You see, what happens inside a man's head is not that he likes you more when he's slept with you. He doesn't think you're so lovely and kind and sweet and such a pleasure to be around. A man thinks that when you are too easy to bed, you will have been too easy for other men too and the perceived value and eligibility that surrounds you will immediately dissipate. The more he has to work hard to win you over, the more he will value you in the long term as a worthwhile and prized possession which he wants to treasure rather than discard.

After the Date

So you've had a wonderful date, you've gone home with a spring in your step, and a smile on your face. You're already wondering whether he felt the same and if he'll contact you. If he's British, it will often be incredibly hard to know whether he actually liked you for the first few dates or whether he was merely being polite and charming in your company. Whether you've been on one date or a few, there are certain things you, as a charming and eligible lady, should really try to avoid doing.

Don't overanalyse

Don't start re-enacting the date in your head as you go to sleep, overanalysing what he meant when he said hello, offered to take your coat, or drove you home. Don't start re-reading his body language and wondering why his legs were uncrossed and facing the door. Don't start thinking that he might have been looking at the pretty blonde girl sitting on the table next to yours. Don't start becoming paranoid that just because he never mentioned doing something again, that he really didn't like you. Don't start worrying about whether your outfit was inappropriate or you were laughing just a little to hard at some of his rather unfunny jokes. In fact, just don' think about the date again once you've left.

Why? Because you have much better things to do than worry about whether he likes you. In fact, he should be so lucky to have a woman like you that if anyone should be worrying it should be HIM. But do you really imagine he will be sitting at home overanalysing things in the way you are now? No, I doubt it. So really, do yourself a favour and stop thinking things through to the point of insanity. The more you overanalyse, the more he's likely to pick up on signals that you're too keen and your perceived eligibility will drop in his eyes.

Don't dissect the date with friends

I know it's rather exciting when we as Brits actually go on these things called 'dates'. We're often so equally excited and disconcerted that we feel we must reassure ourselves before and after the date has taken place by talking through the minute details of the event with those close enough to listen. We want to know what our friends thought of the place he suggested, what he does for a living, when his last relationship ended, what his sense of humour was like, and whether there was any spark. Friends can demand all the details from the first text message to all messages thereafter, and should you encourage it, you can without realising put an immense amount of pressure on yourself. I know that as women we often feel a sense of calm through

If you start gathering other people's opinions before you've had a chance to form your own you may be influenced against liking someone you could grow to love

146

communication. We enjoy sharing our feelings and burdens with friends and family as 'a problem shared is a problem halved'. However, there is a sense that actually often a problem shared, when dealing with something that isn't fundamentally a problem yet and which doesn't really involve anyone else, can actually be a problem exacerbated. You see, when you tell your friends all the details, you are inviting them to give their opinion. If you start gathering other people's opinions before you've had a chance to form your own, you may be influenced against liking someone you could grow to love. Don't involve your friends until you feel you have something to involve them in. You will be doing yourself a favour in the long-term, believe me.

Work out if he's only after one thing

Not all men, as most women learn to realise, are gentlemen. There will invariably be those opportunist-type chaps who are out there to see what they can get away with for as long as possible with as many ladies as possible. These chaps may go on several dates, and be incredibly charming. However, once they have succeeded in winning you over and getting you into bed, they will move onto the next thing that takes their fancy. During the early date phase, therefore, it's always a good idea to try to work out whether your chap may be only after one thing. The Brits, though non-communicative, are often fairly easy to read should they be motivated to get you into bed. In my humble opinion, they will have several of the following traits:

* He had no hesitation in talking to you initially as you may have been one of several ladies he tried his luck

with that evening. Also, often the more a British chap genuinely likes you, the less he is to be confident in approaching you. He may also have been under the influence of alcohol.

*   On your first date he couldn't keep his hands off you. Whilst this is fine when you're officially a couple, it's too much too soon until you get to know one another.

*   He tries to encourage you to go over and watch movies at his house from very early on.

*   He's much more interested in telling you all about how wonderful he is rather than finding out all about you.

*   You never meet his friends, and come to think of it, he doesn't talk about them all that much.

*   He contacts you late in the evening. If you get anything after 9 p.m. or 10 p.m. wanting to meet up that night, ignore him.

*   He contacts you to see you right now, not arrange a specific date in the future.

*   He doesn't actually invite you out but keeps suggesting you go over to his place instead.

*   He starts picture messaging you very early on. Sometimes the photos he sends may be innocent, other times they may be of himself. The reason he's doing this is to encourage you to do the same, so watch out how readily you reciprocate. He may be keen to turn the text chat into sex chat.

*   He might text you, and when you respond, he'll take ages to reply. No doubt the only time you'll get his

interest is if you suggest going over to his place ASAP, in which case he'll reply immediately. Funny that...

* He tells you he doesn't want a girlfriend. If you've gone out with a guy you like a couple of times and he tells you honestly and openly that he doesn't want a girlfriend, then trust me when I say that he won't change his mind. He won't suddenly realise how lovely you are and completely change his tune. He's telling you to manage your expectations so you're really better off believing him.

Don't friend on Facebook

I know we're all often fairly curious people and when we go out with a new person we like, it can be tempting to try to find out as much as we can about them. However, whatever you do, never be the one to initiate befriending your chap on Facebook. Not only do you want to maintain a sense of mystery and intrigue around yourself, but you also don't want to be seen to be that keen to find out about him. By adding him as a friend you are essentially telling him you are interested in him and why should he find out that information without having to work for it? Equally, should a man send you a friend request on Facebook during your early date phase (so within the first two to three dates), you should not accept it until you feel you're in a more committed relationship. It's crucial you don't give too much away too soon. The only time it's okay to accept a friendship on Facebook is when you've been introduced to a chap through mutual friends as, for the

Brits, it can be regarded as rude if you don't accept someone you know from your social circle without good reason.

Just don't call it a date

'Defining an encounter with a female as a 'date' is a bit too explicit, too official, too clear-cut and unambiguous – the sort of embarrassing 'cards on the table' declaration of intent that the naturally cautious, indirect English male prefers to avoid'

A little word to the wise. Although I have just used the term 'date' in this chapter, you really are best placed not banding it about when going on one. It is a word that simply doesn't bode well with most Brits, and whilst people do enjoy the pleasure of each other's company in ways that most other countries would not hesitate to recognise as 'a date' - you might find, if you haven't already, that for Brits making reference to the word creates an awful lot of awkward tension. This is because it scares us Brits and I don't just mean men. Both men and women across the UK have a bit of an aversion to the word 'date'.

It's simply much easier to mask this courting ritual with other less romantic and much less anxiety-inducing words. People will say, 'I'm meeting up with…' 'I'm going for a drink with…' or, 'I've got dinner with this new guy I'm seeing,' as these words do not necessarily imply we might be rejected or let down. A 'date' however, somehow alludes to one person liking the other in a sexual way. But we're British - we don't acknowledge attraction to one another very proficiently as it involves putting our feelings out there, which could be most embarrassing if they didn't like us back. It sounds awfully like their approach to chatting us up doesn't it? There is certainly a common theme of avoiding humiliation that runs very firmly through the psyche of the Brits. Therefore, if he asks you out in his own way, it's probably best to avoid saying what they always appear to say in American movies, and to his suggestion of a coffee you utter 'What, like a date?' (Cringe.)

Kate Fox, in her book 'Watching the English'[3], described it perfectly:

If you have an aversion to the word 'date'

If any of this sounds familiar and you, like many Brits, hate everything about 'dating' (the word, the process, the build-up, the expectation) then rest assured that you are not alone. In fact, most of my clients have a slight aversion to 'dating' in one way or another. Here are a few tips for calming your nerves and helping you to put this whole process into a bit of perspective.

Nobody is testing you, it's not an exam

It's not a test; it's just a normal process. Don't start thinking that just because you're meeting up with someone who has romantic motivations, that you will be expected to behave differently to how you would normally. Just be yourself and don't psyche yourself up too much!

Also, ask yourself why you feel this way. Why do you hate it so much? How does it make you feel? Nobody will be marking you or judging you. It's just a great opportunity to meet somebody new and to increase your social circle. You never know, even if this person isn't going to be quite right for you romantically, you could be lifelong friends!

Remember your confidence

If you're bright, bubbly and confident in most areas of your life, why would you be any different just because he's asked you to join him for a drink? Are you incapable of talking to people who are romantically interested in you? If you do find yourself clamming up at the concept of going out with someone new, you need to consider how you could be sending out mixed messages. If you're charming and confident with everyone else in your life, but go to your date with a face that says, 'I don't want to be here, this is awkward,' not only will your date not think terribly highly of you, but you will go home feeling pretty rotten about yourself too. Remember your confidence, remember your charm and be gracious. The more you smile, the happier you'll feel.

If you hate the word 'date' find another word for it in your head

The power of association is a strong thing. If you get cold sweats thinking about going on a dreaded date, it's very simple – call it something else. Refer to it as a 'drink' or a 'catch-up' or something that sounds a lot less terrifying. If that doesn't work for you, find a good word you're happy with that makes you feel at ease.

A date means really awkward small talk

Well it can. However, if you ask interesting questions you might find it much easier, especially if you can break the ice early with some good banter. Try to set the tone for conversation early on and inject humour, wit and most importantly – don't take yourself too seriously. You need to enjoy the process. It's not meant to be something you endure, it's meant to be fun.

A date means pressure

A lot of the time a date means you haven't been able to find a partner through your friends and social circle. This actually happens quite frequently, especially these days where life has become so individualised and it's harder to meet people. However, that doesn't mean you need to feel pressured. It doesn't matter what comes of it, a lot of the time great dates fail because too much pressure is put on the table. Just relax and be your charming self. If you feel pressure, it will come through and the other party will pick up on it.

A date means you have to get dressed up and make an effort

Why would you want to go to a date looking anything other than the best version of yourself? You are there to let him see how fabulous you are. If you aren't ready to start making an effort to get dressed up, you aren't really open to meeting new people. I understand that if you go on a date a night for several months you might be worn out, but at least you'll look fabulous, right?

What if you don't like each other?

Well, you can't have instant chemistry with everyone, nor can you be everyone's cup of tea, so this WILL happen. That's just the nature of the beast. If you don't like each other, there's no harm in that. In fact, what did you really lose by meeting up with this person? Just keep an open mind, and the more you're open, the more will come your way.

Texting Etiquette

As a nation we love to communicate in as many non-verbal ways as possible. It's simply so much easier to send a text message, an email or buzz someone on WhatsApp than it is to pick up the phone and call them. Calling them is just so emotionally involved. I mean, you have to actually hear their voice! What if they are busy and they can't talk and you've rudely interrupted them? The written message graciously permits you to choose to respond when you're ready, and consider carefully your response. Conversely, a phone call can often make you feel put on the spot as you have to know what to say there and then. There are just so many things to consider when contemplating making a phone call. A non-verbal text message or email seems infinitely easier.

However, as much as we love the convenience of the text message, I think it's fair to say that we as a nation have become somewhat over-reliant on this method of communication. According to Ofcom[4], the SMS peaked as the most popular method of communication in the UK in 2012, and has since (at time of writing in April 2015) been overshadowed by WhatsApp[5]. The sheer number of us now using our smartphones to communicate has increased dramatically. Therefore, for the sake of clarity and to avoid confusion so commonly associated with such written communication, when I refer to 'texting' in this section I'm referring to both traditional SMS messages and WhatsApp conversations.

This over-reliance on 'texting' does tend to have pros and cons when it comes to dating. Whilst it's true that it does enable us to 'hide behind the message' so to speak, whereby we can save ourselves from the awkwardness of having to speak to someone while carefully considering what we want to say, it equally leads us to start overanalysing our responses, deliberating on how long we wait to reply, how long he's taken to text us back and what he really means when he puts one 'x' or two at the end of his message. Not just that, but the nuances of the messages can so easily be misunderstood without the spoken word. Very often, I'll speak to clients who have tried to inject banter or a sense of humour into their messages only to have had them totally misconstrued. Unfortunately, instances like these can make or break a relationship and completely throw off course any chemistry that might have been there during the early date phase.

Therefore, when should or shouldn't you be using and encouraging texting when it comes to dating? What is the best way to text your way to success? Furthermore, what do certain text messages *really* mean when you get them from a guy?

Never initiate

If you quite like a guy, it's not a good idea to initiate contact with him via text as he'll most likely consider you easy prey and will assume he won't have to work that hard to get you, which obviously is not the case for an eligible lady such as yourself. Similarly, if he has initiated contact and has sent you a message or two via SMS, it's not up to you to convert him to communicating with you via WhatsAspp. Wait until he does it himself; otherwise, you're letting him know that you're making yourself more readily available to chat with him. You also don't want to transfer to WhatsApp too soon as you'll ruin some of the intrigue. If they can see you're 'online' and you start 'typing' yet don't press send for ages, you're letting him know you're carefully considering your response, and basically, that you care a little more than perhaps you want to let on.

Keep your responses brief but don't be too cold

If he sends you a message, whatever you do, keep your responses short and sweet and never send more than one message before you hear back from him. Don't be afraid to be friendly in your responses though. British guys don't respond very well to a girl being curt, as they need a little bit more encouragement and will probably just deem it rather blunt and impolite. If a chap texts you to find out what day of the week you're free to catch up for a drink, don't reply saying something like 'It's a really busy week. Maybe Wed'. Instead, make sure he knows you're still keen to a point, so say something like 'A drink sounds great. What a hectic week. Wed works for me!' Although you're essentially saying the same thing, there's no need to respond in a way that could be misconstrued as impolite.

Limit yourself to one kiss

This is a much-debated topic, but I personally think that there's no harm in ending your message with either one kiss or your initials and a kiss, so long as you are consistent with it in the early stages. If you don't put a kiss on the end of your message it could be misconstrued as a bit too unfriendly for us Brits, and imply that you take yourself a little too seriously. If he doesn't put a kiss at the end of his message when he initiates, don't worry and don't read too much into it. You can still put a kiss on the end of your message without him thinking you're a stalker. It also implies you haven't over-analysed his message and noticed he didn't put a kiss on the end. In fact, I bet if you do he'll message you back with a kiss too going forward. Whatever you do though don't start feeling encouraged by his contact and adding more and more kisses to your text messages the more you like him. It's not really necessary and what you're saying via your message should be found in the words rather than the X at the end.

Don't use too many Smilies and Emojis

The same can be said for the use of Smilies and Emojis when texting. Please do try to limit your use of them to no more than one if you need to include them in a message. Whilst they can often help convey when you're joking (smiley face) and being cheeky (giggle), you don't want to seem like you're incapable of actually using the English language. An elegant and demure lady such as yourself is perfectly capable of communicating without the aid of multiple cartoon characters.

Grammar and spelling

Some of my personal bug-bears are the use of abbreviated words via text message and incorrect spelling. Be gracious enough to write the whole word for 'you' and 'are' and hopefully he'll reciprocate. If he writes you anything along the lines of 'wot u up to L8ter?' I would carefully reconsider going on a date with the chap. Also, if you're in need of brushing up on your spelling and grammar and can't remember the difference between 'there', 'they're' and 'their', or 'to' and 'too', it's not a bad idea to do a quick read through of your message before pressing send, as spelling mistakes in text messages can be a big turn off for both men and women. If you're looking for an intelligent, educated chap, he's probably looking for the same.

Don't be overfamiliar

If his name is John, during the early dates you're best advised to refer to him as John. Do not start being over-familiar and start your messages with 'Hey sweetie' or 'Hey handsome'. It's just too much too soon and you'll probably look a little too keen.

Don't encourage the booty call text

A lot of guys try their luck. If you ever get a text from a man rather late in the evening, it's probably because he's only got one thing on his mind. If this does happen and you get a text when you're about to get ready for bed along the lines of, 'Can't wait to see you soon,' or even, 'Sleep well,' don't respond as he's probably just trying to see how far he can get. Next thing you know if you do, he'll be suggesting he misses you and wants to come over and see you. Make sure you set boundaries with him so he knows to be respectful and treat you the way you deserve to be treated.

Don't wait hours to respond, be realistic

I don't believe in a specific formula for how long you should wait to respond to a text, but be realistic. In today's day and age, we all have our smartphones practically tied to our hips, so taking a full day to respond isn't really acceptable and will only give off the impression that you're playing games. As a consequence, as soon as you start playing games, it's very likely that so will he. You don't want to get into a mode of 'text tennis' when you're both waiting longer than the other to respond so as to not seem too keen. This is not only incredibly boring, but it's really frustrating for both parties involved, as nobody ever really says what they mean. Furthermore, a lot of relationships can fail to get off the ground if this happens, as one or both parties can often lose interest if it all seems like too much hard work.

Don't text him if you get no reply

If he doesn't reply to you, even if you send a message that didn't' warrant a reply, do not text him again. For example, let's say he texts you on Monday morning to find out how your weekend was. You reply with 'Yeah it was really good thanks. Monday blues!' Your message didn't necessarily ask a question or denote a response, but that doesn't mean you should send another message as you feel guilty that you could have come across as rude or curt. Whilst I don't believe British men respond well to the old rules of treat them mean and keep them keen, you certainly don't need to do anything to appear too keen either. If you message him before he's replied, what you're essentially doing in his mind is checking he's still interested and giving him the impression you're keen to hear from him.

However, you are an eligible lady, so you have an awful lot going on in your life, which is far more important than worrying about whether he's interested or when he will text back. He should be lucky to have you! If he's keen he'll reply, so let him come to you, as the more you're seen to be chasing him, the less he will start to value you.

Don't text after a few drinks

It's very easy for emotions to become more heightened after a few drinks and for the British reserve to become, well, somewhat unreserved. We start to relax and let our inhibitions liquefy further into every glass of wine we drink. Although drinking responsibly is, of course, a huge part of British culture (as is drinking irresponsibly these days, but I'm sure you ladies don't fall into that category), it's important not to let the false sense of confidence get the better of you. When you're out with your friends and having a few drinks, resist the urge to message your chap and find out what he's doing. Certainly don't ever initiate trying to meet up if you're out with your friends. You'll only be giving off the impression that you can't really have fun without him there.

If you can't control yourself and you have a bad habit of drunk texting, then give your phone to a friend who will be responsible for it for you.

Never declare your feelings by text message

I know we're bad at communicating as a nation, but please leave the ground-breaking feelings for when you meet in person. There's nothing worse than using a text message to tell people that a) You have feelings for them b) You love them c) You want to dump them.

Don't let texting go on and on

The whole point of texting should not be to replace verbal communication entirely. If a guy is entirely incapable of communicating with you in any way other than texting and you've been out with him a couple of times, then you do need to encourage him to give you a call. Say things like, 'I miss your voice,' or, 'I can't wait to talk to you soon,' to encourage them to pick up the phone. What's more, texting should be used predominantly as a medium to ask you out again or arrange to see you again, not for exchanging sweet nothings without some action. So don't let him stall and faff about not getting to the point. If a guy is just writing one message after the other without a clear objective (i.e. another date in the diary) then you should probably cool off a bit until he does. Don't give him the impression that it's acceptable by writing equally long messages back. You should aim to write back much shorter and more punctual messages so he starts to realise he needs to up his game.

www.sovainbooks.co.uk/texting

Taking Things To The Next Level

Stepping it up

So it's all been going rather swimmingly. You've been on a few dates with a guy you like, and you rather suspect he likes you too. You're keen for things to develop as he's certainly piqued your interest. So far, he's been treating you well and promptly following up after each date to schedule the next one. Contact has been regular and you don't feel like any games are being played. In fact, you really start to look forward to hearing from him. Great, it finally happened, you think you might have met a good one!

After you get through the early dates, the next few months can often be the most exciting, as both parties relax and really enjoy the process of getting to know one another. It's actually often during this phase that the British man excels himself and can actually be much more romantic, as he's got over the jitters of initial communication and starts to build confidence in your relationship. He may suggest a weekend trip away, or book a romantic treat to show you what a great potential partner he can be.

It's important you use the next few months wisely, as you're going to need to be fairly disciplined in determining whether this chap is *Mr Right* or *Mr Right Now*. It's easy during this phase of rapture to get carried away with the chemistry and the feeling of euphoria that comes with being attracted to someone, and sensing they feel the same way back. You need to be very strategic in trying to not only work out what kind of character you're dealing with, but also whether his motivations match yours.

Don't Rush it

Don't rush this period, take your time to enjoy getting to know one another before pushing things to develop. You will be much better placed pacing the relationship evenly and keeping your space so as to keep the excitement going for as long as possible. If he's the one pushing to see you more often, then don't feel bad about being too busy to see him every now and then. He will only keep finding you more interesting so don't let your novelty wear off too soon. If you do see each other often, and have got into the habit of staying over at each other's houses, then take note of how many times you've had a night to yourself. It's important that you are not seen to be super keen to move into his place yet or make any notions you're pushing for marriage. You don't want to spoil a good thing by rushing it along too early on. So do enjoy this period, but be mindful to keep things on an even keel and not get carried away.

Keep your own life

When they're not with their budding beau during this stage, some women start to get jittery about where their man might be. Is he going out with his friends and meeting other people? What did he do this weekend without me? Who is that woman in the photo he's tagged with on Facebook? Don't start overanalysing and panicking about the status of your new relationship, just relax and ensure you keep your life as busy and as full as it was before you met him. So stick to the plans you make with your friends, don't be seen to cancel anything just because he's come on the scene. The more he feels like you are prioritising him, the less he's likely to prioritise you, so be sure to maintain your independence. Also, don't wait for him to suggest what you're going to do with your weekend. Make your own plans and tell him what you're up to. Your life should never revolve around him, you're far too valuable for that. Besides, men find it terribly unattractive if you're seen to rely on them too much. You had your own life before you met him, so why should that stop just because he's come on the scene. My mother always told me, 'Never rely on a man or a trust fund as both could run out!' and she was right!

Beware the man who comes on strong

Very often strong women will be lured in by what I call the 'Come on Strong Man'. If a chap comes on too strong too fast, then beware that you need to be the one to put the brakes on. Time and time again this is a man who you may initially have needed some persuading to date, as you weren't all that convinced there was any chemistry there, but once you did start dating him you became overwhelmed and flattered by how much he appeared to be into you and your relationship. Therefore, you suddenly found yourself being convinced to rush things along at a pace you probably wouldn't have felt comfortable with had it been anyone else.

If you feel as though you've come across a chap like this, don't let him convince you to get carried away with things if you instinctively feel they are moving too fast. Often women will set out to be clear and logical in a new relationship, and aim to take things slowly, only to have a guy be really persuasive and try and keep the relationship moving at pace. What tends to happen is an unfortunate cycle. The woman, who was initially fairly sceptical, starts to feel flattered by his enthusiasm so she lets it continue. Things might go really well at first, which make her then start to relax into the relationship and believe that, because he's coming on so strong, he must be serious. Unfortunately, only then does the chap start to realise he's now won you over and you're expecting him to live up to all the things he's been promising. Guess what, he's out of there faster than you can say 'Commitaholic'.

Yes, the 'Come on Strong Man' is unfortunately so keen to win you over, but terrified of committing to you, and he can leave a trail of disaster behind him as you try to make sense of what happened. If you suspect you might be faced with such a character, watch out for the following signs:

* He seems to love the thrill of the chase and worked hard to win you over.
* He suggested having an exclusive relationship with you quickly, only after a few dates.
* He will tell you how amazing you are and flatter you constantly.
* He may have had a string of short-term relationships but doesn't really talk about them.
* He will chase when you pull away, and retract when you're keen.

* He has a job that enables him to travel for quite a lot of the time.

Don't start trying too hard

Just because you're going steady and enjoying each other's company does not mean that you suddenly go over and above the call of duty, bending over backwards to please him. Women often feel, perhaps because they might have been single for a while, that when they do find a nice guy they really want to keep him. They love the feeling of happiness, of intimacy, of waking up together and having lazy Sunday mornings reading the newspapers – so they feel that by making him happy, he will stay close.

Unfortunately, men are often the opposite, especially in the early days when you're still getting to know one another. They are still keen to value you and place you on a pedestal, as they want the eligible woman they are with to continue to behave like one to make them feel they have won a wonderful catch. Therefore, if you start finding yourself cooking him a loving dinner followed by breakfast in bed the following morning, and you popping out first thing to get the milk for his tea while he's still sleeping – think again. He will not find it endearing, only a little pathetic. He will not be thinking how lovely you are, only what else he will be able to get away with. The more you try to please, the more he will feel he can get away with, so be sure to set your relationship boundaries cautiously during this phase of your relationship. You do not want him to start taking advantage of your character.

Work out his character

When you're getting to know one another and things are stepping up a gear, an important step people often overlook is really trying to get to the core of the type of character you're dealing with. If you can get a sense of what motivates your chap, what scares him and what inspires him, you can be better placed to know how to react accordingly.

By this I don't mean that you have to change who you are or how you behave around him. Goodness knows eligible ladies such as yourselves would never be seen to lower themselves to change for a man. What it does give us, however, is knowledge, and knowledge is power. It also enables you to recognise certain character traits to look out for in your guy that you are likely to be more or less suited to.

These are tips I often coach my clients when I match them up with potential partners. If you have a sense of what makes your guy tick, what currency he deals in, what motivates him and inspires him - you are giving yourself the upper hand by being able to know how to respond. Understanding their personality and character enables you to do what psychologists call 'slotting', which means you can work out how you and he could be fundamentally compatible. You'll also be less surprised by certain actions on his part if you understand why he does them.

So if he doesn't call straight away, you can start to understand why. If he has to do things his way or wants YOU to decide on where to go for the date, you may know the reason for it. Using basic psychological analysis called 'Personality Temperaments

Theory'[6], you can start to work out characteristics of both you and your date. So, what are the key character traits to look out for? Put a tick against which of the following statements best describe a recent date you went on:

1) *Before the date...*
   a) He booked the date well in advance and organised everything (D)
   b) He organised the date and was keen to tell you about the good reviews he had read about it online (T)
   c) Before booking anything he offered you the choice of where to go or asked if you knew of somewhere nice (F)
   d) He didn't organise the date that well in advance but when he did he made sure he got you one of the hottest tables in town (A)

2) *When you talked about the future...*
   a) He talked about his plans for the future quite a bit and all the pretty impressive things he wanted to achieve (A)
   b) He didn't talk in detail but, but when he did he actually brought up what happened in the past more than the future (T)
   c) He didn't talk about himself that much, he mostly asked me about what I had planned for the future rather than talk about himself (F)
   d) He wasn't keen to discuss the future. He talked about the night itself, commented a lot on the food (D)

3) What was your first impression of him?
   a) He seemed to be relaxed and conversation flowed easily (F)
   b) He knew immediately exactly what he wanted to eat and was quite direct with the staff (D)
   c) He was really funny and incredibly enthusiastic about the date (A)
   d) He was quite reserved and seemed to be analysing his surroundings on the date quite a bit (T)

4) What was the conversation like?
   a) He asked loads of questions but I did most of the talking, either way the conversation never seemed to stop and we got on really well (F)
   b) He talked a lot about his achievements and his job most of the time, all sounded pretty impressive if not a bit over the top at times (A)
   c) He asked a lot of questions about my past and the choices I'd made in an analytical way, he really wanted to get to know me (T)
   d) He was engaging but kept his phone on the table in case he got work emails, which led me to believe that work was super important to him (D)

5) Your overall opinion of him was...
   a) He was very respectful and kind (F)
   b) He was polite, reserved and often a bit hesitant (T)
   c) He was pretty insistent and kind of direct at times (D)
   d) He certainly had a lot of opinions but was interesting and expressive (A)

6) *After the date...*

a) He calls or texts soon after the date and gets something else scheduled in soon (D)

b) Before you leave your date he mentions a busy weekend he's got with his friends and is a bit ambiguous about when and if he'll be in touch (A)

c) He'll say it was really nice to meet you, he had a great time and he's got your number. He might even reach in for the kiss (F)

d) He texts soon after the date to say he hopes you enjoyed the date, he specifically enjoyed the scallops (T)

7) *Now you've been on a few dates, how do you feel your relationship is progressing?*

a) He's taking things slowly, and keen to analyse things properly before jumping in, he's always asking me lots of questions (T)

b) You get on really well, but you never know how he feels as he's not terribly open and often doesn't really talk about himself (F)

c) He's keen and he lets me know it. He's always booking the next thing we can do together (D)

d) He's enthusiastic and I like him. I'm just taking things with a pinch of salt as I've noticed he likes to exaggerate (A)

RESULTS

Most people will have more of certain character traits than others. Work out which of the below best reflects your chap.

Majority of A's – The Actor
Majority of D's – The Doer
Majority of T's – The Thinker
Majority of F's – The Friend

The Actor

The Actor has a mission to be in charge and loves to control things with flair and panache so will tend to inject a bit of style into what he does. They are really good at creating strong mental pictures when they tell stories and are innovative, so they tend to make natural leaders as people enjoy being in their company. Give them an audience and they are happy; however, put them on their own and they can lose their energy and become somewhat introspective. The key thing about the actor is that he loves to feel acknowledged and recognised, so you'll often find him going to the trendiest bars and restaurants 'to be seen' buying prestigious things such as fine food and wine and the latest gadgets. If you date an Actor he's inevitably the kind of guy to shower you with gifts at the beginning and will want to impress you by taking you to the hottest restaurants in town. However, as much as they may be keen to impress you on a date, they can also be guilty of monopolising the conversation and making it all about them, so you might find yourself listening to stories of their achievements and generally feeling like they themselves are their favourite topic of conversation. Don't expect them to ask you too many questions, but do be prepared to listen attentively to what they say and take a really keen interest in them. The more you are seemingly charmed and impressed by an Actor, the more they will find you charming and attractive, so don't try to shift the conversation back around to yourself if they are in their swing. An Actor will enjoy the process of taking the lead so is very likely to book and arrange the date, often without too much notice, as it's hugely exciting for him to be spontaneous.

Key characteristics of an actor:
* They have a fun personality, often very magnetic and charming.
* Avid storytellers and good with words.
* Spontaneous and enthusiastic about life.
* Love to feel valued and recognised, and excel with an audience.
* They immediately make you feel at ease in their company.
* Sociable and popular, often with a large group of friends.

Good tips when dating an actor
* Play to his ego. You're really going to want to show how impressed you are by everything about him in order to get in his good books. If you're out on a date, mention things that you find particularly impressive such as 'Oh, my God, this is the nicest cocktail I've

ever had' or 'you really did book the very best table, I'm impressed!'

* If you're a chatty kind of girl, you're going to really want to brush up on your listening skills, as an actor likes to do the talking. If you dominate the conversation, he will feel like he's not being recognised and that he's not getting a chance to show you how amazing he is.

* They often have high energy and are enthusiastic, so be sure to match their style. Be lively and stimulating and he'll respond positively.

* An Actor isn't detail-oriented so you're best not mentioning it if he's telling a story that is perhaps not one hundred per cent factually correct, it will irritate him. Just let it go and turn a blind eye rather than picking him up on the details and correcting him.

* Actors really respond well to people inspiring them to achieve greater things, so listen enthusiastically to what he has to say and encourage him to strive for the best.

* An actor may want to date someone who they think improves their lives, and their reputation, so the more you give off the impression that you're a high-value, eligible woman, the more he will be enamoured by you.

Watch out for:
* They can be pretty inconsistent as they will change their tune to suit who they are talking to or 'their audience'.

* They are likely to be slightly overzealous with the truth and can exaggerate so as to impress so might be guilty of a few false truths every now and then.
* An actor often has loads of energy to start something, but that can tail off pretty quickly so be mindful when getting romantically involved.
* They can be pretty superficial and may want to date someone who they think improves their lives, and their reputation, so he won't necessarily be led by his feelings.
* Can often bore easily and would rather detach themselves from a relationship than lose self-esteem.
* Watch out for their charm! They love to be in control so can be fairly manipulative, especially when it comes to talking you into something.

The Friend

The Friend values himself through his ability to form great relationships, and so the main currency they deal in is trust. Knowing you can be trusted and have high morals and integrity are of key importance when dating a Friend, and they might be keen to mention how they feel, or felt about certain things in their lives. Therefore, unlike the Actor, who values prestige, the Friend is more concerned with reliability. The Friend is the type of guy who is likely to have photos of his family on his phone or at home, but none of himself. These men are incredibly loyal and really care deeply about how the other person feels. Therefore, when on a date with a Friend, he is very likely to ask you loads of questions about you and divert the conversation away from himself as much as possible, as he wants to build rapport and get along with people. Whilst you may enjoy being in the company of a Friend, and have had the impression that the date has gone really well, you need to watch out for how much he felt engaged, as it's very possible you might have enjoyed the date much more than he did. A Friend would never want to let you know he wasn't enjoying himself, as he is sympathetic to your feelings. The Friend is easy going, relaxed and really good at listening, but he can often keep his emotions hidden and be pretty indecisive about things. He might not be the kind of guy to have a date organised, preferring instead to ask you what you would like to do, as he'd be afraid to disappoint you and make a poor decision.

Key characteristics of a Friend
* They tend to be very relaxed and informal.
* Great at listening.
* Supportive and respectful.
* Will get along with everyone and great at building rapport.
* Humble and, where possible, avoid confrontation.
* Caring and collaborative, will want to involve you.
* They like to get on with others rather than cause conflict.
* They love developing relationships and building trust.
* Not a huge fan of new ideas and change.
* Can be slow to make decisions and fairly indirect in what they mean.
* Least likely to click with a 'Doer'.

Good tips when dating a Friend

* Show that you're trustworthy and have good morals, that you would never cheat and believe in doing the right thing.
* Don't be too formal, it will only make them uncomfortable.
* Focus on the positive, be enthusiastic.
* Mention anything you've done that has helped others.
* They love to be involved, so ask them what they think about things.
* Brush up on a bit of small talk as this makes the Friend characters feel more comfortable and is their way of forming relationships.
* Often likes to have approval so be sure to comment on his good choice of date venue or choice of meal/drink if you go out somewhere.
* Be patient and give them time, they're not driven by urgency.

Watch out for:

* You'll end up doing most of the talking as he'll like to ask about you, but watch out you don't bore him. If you do he'll never let you know it, but probably will just ignore calling you again for a second date. Friends would rather sacrifice honestly for harmony, so beware!
* Friends don't like to talk about themselves so you'll rarely feel you know what's going on inside them. They also have a tendency to agree with you so be

sure to ask him lots of questions, although it's best not to get too deep.

* Watch your body language, as he'll feel uncomfortable with inexpressive eye contact and a closed expression.

* Don't criticize others or speak badly about anyone. Friends hate conflict, so hold back on telling that story about your ex-boyfriend or how upset you are with your friend at the moment.

* As ironic as the name implies, it's easy to get in to the friend zone when dealing with a Friend. You have to up your flirtation skills a little with them, in order to put yourself on a level different to everyone else he meets and talks to. Be really expressive with your eyes and body language so he knows you're interested romantically.

* Friends don't like to take control, so don't expect him to feel that comfortable making any big moves without significant encouragement.

* He might reach for a kiss at the end of the date as he's keen for you to like him, but don't read too much into this unless his future actions back this behaviour up.

* Friends can be pretty indecisive and 'wishy washy', so they might not be keen to jump into a relationship right away. Don't rush them, let them come to the decision on their own.

* They tend to live very much in the moment, so the furthest they will be comfortable talking about until you know them better is the week ahead. Certainly don't bring up discussions on marriage or babies until later down the line.

* They can procrastinate and do tomorrow what could be done today.

The Doer

The Doer is at his most comfortable when he's being efficient and getting things done, and the currency he tends to deal in is time. He's the type of character who will book things well in advance and has a diary full of not just meetings for work, but social occasions too. He will be happy buying tickets as soon as they become available for his favourite sport matches or music concerts, as he feels motivated by knowing when something is taking place and being well informed. When you're on a date with a Doer, he loves to be organised and in control, so it's likely he would have booked something without necessarily asking for any advice. However, a conversation with a Doer might feel slightly stilted, as they are not as good at building rapport as the Actor or Friend. In fact, you might have the impression they stopped paying attention when you were telling a story. This is because the Doer is motivated by getting to the point quickly, so you'll want to be mindful how long you spend telling the joke before getting to the punch line, so to speak. A Doer is strong willed, decisive and values efficiency in the people around him, so don't be too late or mention how you love to laze about in your PJ's on a Sunday afternoon. He might be slightly intolerant of such behaviour until you get to know him. They can also seem fairly non-empathetic and cold, but in reality they are just trying to avoid wasting valuable time when they could be achieving their goals. This is why text messages or phone calls from a Doer will be short and sweet, often to the point of curt.

Key Characteristics of a Doer
* Believes nothing is impossible and very goal-oriented.
* Very spontaneous and decisive.
* They know exactly what they want and how to get there.
* Likely to be organised and book things well in advance.
* Dynamic and active.
* Task-oriented rather than a 'people person'.
* Loves to be independent and self-sufficient.
* Like to move at a fast pace, quick to make decisions.
* Direct and to the point.
* Not very good at listening as he wants to control the conversation; he may interrupt.
* Least likely to click with a 'Friend'.

Good tips when dating a Doer
* If they are interested in you, they will pursue you like a goal and will do what it takes to win you over. Be aware that their interest might not last forever, though, as they value efficiency and getting things done swiftly.
* Don't try to establish control over your dates with a Doer. Let him choose where to go and book the arrangements as he may not enjoy sitting in the passenger seat.
* Don't waffle on endlessly with your stories. Keep things short and sweet so as to not bore him.
* Try not to be too indecisive around him. If you're out for dinner and don't know what to order, rather than

just say, 'Oh, I don't know what I fancy' it's better to give him options to work with as he's solution driven. So say, 'Hmm, I'm torn between the risotto or the fish.'

* Don't take it personally that he can be abrupt and direct, especially if you're a Friend yourself. Just recognise this different personality type is motivated differently.
* Likes to talk very fast so make sure you're listening attentively to what he has to say; otherwise, he'll get impatient with your inefficiency.
* Tends to have a body language that leans in towards who he is talking to, so be sure to respond accordingly if you're interested.

Watch out for:
* He can be deemed as slightly blunt in the way he communicates so text messages or phone calls may be short and sweet, often to the point of rude.
* Might not appreciate feeling out-accomplished, so if you're also a Doer yourself, be mindful of not shouting about your achievements too early on.
* They don't like to be told what to do and what not to do, so be careful of suggesting where to go or what to do so as to make them not feel in control.
* Can be very inflexible, dominant and demanding.
* Might give off the impression they don't need friends so can seem quite cold as they control their emotions very well.
* Two Doers may clash.

The Thinker

The Thinker is exceptionally analytical and loves to have all information available to help him make a decision. They would rather get something done right than get it done quickly and so, on dates, can often take his time to ask lots of questions, gathering information, which they then revel in processing so as to determine whether or not you both get on. Thinkers are very disciplined and organised, but often come across as quite serious and indirect. They are good at listening, yet they may often not appear to be, as they don't tend to give much away in terms of body language, so will make limited gestures and potentially appear quite hesitant and reserved. Although you won't necessarily feel like you've build a good rapport on a date with a Thinker, you will feel as though he's made a concerted effort to get to know you due to the sheer volume of questions he may have thrown your way. Often these are questions that nobody else would ask, as he's very perceptive. The Thinker is so good at being analytical and spotting the gaps, so he may try to work out your character and make sense of who you are. On a date, he may comment on the particulars of the evening such as the food or wine, and might seem quite critical of the service. He's likely to have read reviews of various restaurants online and will be keen to tell you why the one he's selected is the best in his opinion. Thinkers will love to engage in a good conversation, maybe a discussion or debate to get them considering things from all sides. Be careful though, as a Thinker loves to be right, and if you don't give him all the facts, he can often have a selective hearing until you do. They can be quite stubborn and obtuse.

Key Characteristics of a Thinker
*   Love to gather data and will ask a lot of questions to get to know you.
*   Detail-oriented, slow at making decisions.
*   Good at listening but can often come across as quite sceptical and critical.
*   Relationships are important, but only second to facts
*   They love predictability and routine.
*   Love to be right so can often seem stubborn or inflexible
*   Fascinated with the process of achieving something rather than actually achieving it.

Good Tips when dating a Thinker
*   Most likely to clash with a Friend, who they'll see as overly familiar and wishy washy.
*   Feel free to provide a Thinker with a lot of information. They love to discuss things so will revel in a thoughtful debate or discussion.
*   They don't necessarily move quickly, so might take some time to process where you are in the relationship or analyse thoughts and feelings.
*   Try to ensure what you say is clear and logical to avoid a Thinker being frustrated.
*   They might appear unenthusiastic but don't confuse that with disinterest.
*   Likes to concentrate on one thing at a time, so makes a loyal partner.
*   They do tend to enjoy the thrill of the chase though, as they are fascinated by the journey rather than the end goal, so be mindful of that when dating a Thinker.

When are you actually officially a couple?

A funny thing often happens when we Brits start dating. Despite it all going so well, it's hard to know the exact moment that the transition takes place between simply 'going out' and becoming an 'official couple', so to speak. The Brits don't like to put their feelings on the line until they know it's safe to do so; therefore, raising the notion of being a couple can often be deemed as hard, if not harder than actually saying 'I love you'. They need to feel confident in the relationship and one hundred per cent convinced the other person feels the same before they will venture forth!

So what are women meant to do when they get to this point with their budding beau, and they want to take things forward? It does very much depend on the dynamic of your relationship as I'm sure you'll agree, and I would never assume all chaps are the same. However, in my humble opinion, it's best to approach things with the following things in mind.

Make sure it's what you want

You might really like this guy and are feeling excited, but just be sure you have considered what you are getting yourself into before you get too involved. Perhaps only recently did you get over a breakup and you're not emotionally ready, or maybe you're still working out whether you're that keen. Don't waste your time, or his, by trying to get to the point of being in a relationship unless you have it very clear in your heart that it's what you want. Without sounding too melodramatic, I'm afraid decisions such as these are best left to the heart and not the mind, so if you're trying to decide on this from a rational perspective, it probably means you're not feeling strongly enough about him.

If it is what you want, never let him know

If you're sure you want to get involved with this chap, then that's great, but never be too keen to let him know you want to be his 'girlfriend'. It's important that you give him something to strive for and he's got to have the sense that you are a prized possession. Therefore, hinting that you're keen to become an official couple will only make you lose some of your intriguing lustre, as you're basically saying he's got you already. Make sure you're giving off the impression that you have an awful lot going on, that you are a highly sought after lady in all areas of your life, and that so far you are just enjoying his company.

If you've been dating a guy for a while and are starting to get a little frustrated or impatient with his inability to refer to you as his girlfriend when, for all intents and purposes, you are – then don't put up with it. I have met some men who will happily see a girl for months if not years and they'll never refer to her as their girlfriend. If this happens, I'm afraid to say it's a clear indication that the chap isn't really invested in you or the relationship, and he's getting what he needs out of it without making the necessary commitments. It also implies he's on the hunt for the next best thing whenever he finds it, so save yourself from the potential heartbreak and move on. If, however, you're both happy with the status quo and expectations are agreed, then that's fine, but don't wait around for a guy to change and wake up one day wanting to be in a committed relationship with you. If he's not keen to tie you down, he's not that keen in general.

Don't mention it before he does

The more dates you go on, the more comfortable you'll inevitably feel around each other, and the easier it will be to bring up topics of conversation surrounding commitment. You might have discussed thoughts on marriage and children over dinner one night, which is absolutely fine. However, no matter how comfortable you both feel talking about such topics, don't misconstrue the situation and bring up the notion of you and him being a 'couple' before he does. The man should want to bring it up because he should want it to happen, and he needs to come to this decision without any pressure from you, so if he feels he is in any way influenced into making this decision, he'll probably back off.

If he does mention it, it's no big deal

So, if and when he does finally bring up the notion of being 'exclusive' in whichever way he does it – and often Brits can be quite unremarkable by how they approach the topic – it does not mean you should start crying tears of joy or hugging him so tightly whilst shuddering with relief. Should a gentleman be keen to have an exclusive relationship with you, all you need to respond is something along the lines of, 'I think that sounds lovely, let's take it slow and see how we go'. This implies that you're in no way applying any pressure to the situation and that there's still some work involved from his side to convince you.

Now there are some caveats to consider here. Whilst the British man loves a drink, should he be under the influence of alcohol when he starts motioning towards this topic (as can often be the case), then think carefully how to respond. Although often alcohol can induce true feelings, it can also lead to feelings being artificially heightened. Consider the dynamic of your relationship up until that point if that happens. If the guy brings it up when you're still on your first or second drink, that's totally acceptable, but if several drinks later he suddenly starts proclaiming how strong his feelings are for you – beware. You might not want to reciprocate fully until you're both on sober ground.

Meeting the Friends/Parents

When you have been going out with a chap for a while, there will inevitably come a time when you will have to meet the friends and, thereafter, all being well, the parents. British men can often feel rather uncomfortable with this concept until they are sure you are set to be a permanent fixture, as they will inevitably receive several lines of questioning from all involved as to the gravity of the relationship. Therefore, it's crucial for this reason that when the notion of introducing each other to the important people in your lives comes about, it is very much led by the man first. He must be the one to suggest it without any pressure from you. If a man feels pressured into progressing a relationship at a pace he is not comfortable with, he may start to cool, and being British he probably won't tell you what's wrong – he'll simply go quiet on you. Let him be the one to initiate meeting any friends and parents well before you do. What's more, when he does suggest it, don't be too enthusiastic about the encounter. Make sure you let him know you may have plans but you'll check your diary, and all being well, the idea sounds nice.

Don't let yourself get stuck in a tricky situation either, like my friend Emily did. She had been seeing a guy for a short period of time when he suggested they join some of his friends to go to the Henley Regatta that year. Having grown up around the Henley area, Emily thought it sounded like a lovely idea, and she coincidentally had friends going that same day too. On the day, her date graciously introduced Emily to his friends and equally when they bumped into her friends a short while later he was charming and polite when meeting them too, so they stayed and had a few drinks. Emily thought things were going really well as everyone seemed to be getting on famously. A few drinks turned into hours spent with her friends rather than his. As the day drew on, Emily and her man started discussing how to make their way back to London where they both lived. He had previously arranged a taxi with his friends to take a large group of them back at once, but when the time came to leave, he couldn't find any of them. After a few investigative phone calls it turned out the group they had arrived with had already left without them! It was at this point that Emily suggested they just go back to her parents' house, which wasn't far from where they were in Henley. The chap suddenly felt hugely uneasy and insisted they go back to London by taxi on their own. The atmosphere from that point forth could have been cut with a knife, as unfortunately Emily had overstepped the mark in terms of making undue introductions. What had started as him introducing her to his friends, became very much more weighted towards her making the introductions. Whilst it was fine for him to meet a couple who were coincidentally there on the day and spend some time with them, the chap didn't really appreciate being taken away from his friends for so long, and then seemingly being made to meet the parents.

Therefore, should a man offer to introduce you to his friends, you should be gracious and spend the time with them even if you have friends present. It's perhaps best not to bring up meeting the parents until sometime after that too, and only once he has suggested it first.

Saying 'I love you'

It's exciting when you're both infatuated with each other. You stare deeply into each other's eyes and see nobody else in the room. Time flies and all you want to do is spend time together. You are lovingly holding hands wherever you go and all you can think about is what the future might hold. That's what you're thinking right?

Well, to a guy, it's a pretty different thought process. Men do not think about relationships in the same way women do. That's not to say that they are not important to men, they are, but men feel more driven by knowing you value them than feeling valued themselves. You see, for a man, uttering or hearing these three words can make him start to question whether he's losing his freedom, whether he can ever truly provide this woman with happiness and love, or whether he's really ready to commit. We, as women, don't think about it this way as we feel secure when we hear the words, and we feel our relationship has been given a seal of approval of sorts. However, a man can often feel quite the opposite unless he's completely convinced and besotted with his lady.

British men can be frustratingly difficult in this regard. One of my previous clients was seeing a gorgeous lady for about four months, and all had been going really well. He had introduced her to his friends, she was taken to Scotland to meet his family and everyone gave glowing reports that this was the first lady he had ever been so serious about. So, when I called him up to ask him how it was going and whether he'd said the three words yet his reply was, 'No, but she hasn't said them to me either, so I'm not going to say it first.'

I was shocked. When it comes to saying, 'I love you,' who should be the one to say it first?

British men, as we know by now, are very non-communicative, and my client was a prime example of how hard he found it to express himself. For all intents and purposes it was plain to see he was very much in love with the lady he was seeing, but telling her how he felt was incredibly difficult. Despite this, however, it's still crucial that the words come from *him* first. You see, because the words intrinsically imply a pressure of sorts to a man that they don't to a lady, he's got to be ready to get there on his own. If you say it first, you're essentially encouraging him to reciprocate or else create problems in your relationship. You don't want a man to say it back because he feels he should, you want a man to say it back because he feels strongly enough to say it. If, like my client, he simply wants you to say it first, then let him wait. He needs to man up and realise you're an eligible lady with plenty of potential suitors who would be dying to be in his shoes. You don't tell him you love him until he's said it first.

If he does, congratulations. To a British guy this usually is a pretty big deal (unless of course he says it drunk or after only two dates in an attempt to get you into bed, then it's safe to say it's probably not 'love' he's feeling).

It Doesn't End There

You're now comfortably calling each other girlfriend and boyfriend or partner, and are, without screaming it from the rooftops, a proper couple. Things have progressed nicely, you've met the parents, he's said he loves you and you are so beyond yourself with excitement that you've found what appears to be a good egg. You might have gone on a few romantic trips together or attended weddings, and now friends are starting to comment on what a great couple you make and whether or not he might be marriage material. So, if you want to get to the 'M' word, how do you keep his interest peaked without piling on any undue pressure that we know British chaps so often clam up when faced with?

Never stop making him miss you

Just because you're a couple doesn't mean you can't still create a bit of push-pull tension. Let him see you, but then let him miss you. If you're talking to him on the phone, make sure you suggest hanging up before he does and try not to accept any last minute dates just because he happens to be free and get home early from work. Let him continue to realise that you have your own life and your own independence, with or without him.

Be spontaneous

Guys love it when they get treated every once in a while. Whilst the early date phase should be predominantly filled with him trying to woo you over and treating you, during this phase it doesn't hurt to plan a surprise trip for him every once in a while to do something he'll love. This could be anything from going to his favourite sports match together, planning a romantic weekend in the country, or sending him for that massage he's needed for so long for his sore back from long hours at the office. It also doesn't hurt to plan a few extra saucy treats for your man during this phase. Find out what his favourite lingerie is and surprise him by wearing it. The more spontaneous you are, the less he feels like your life together is going to be a boring routine, the more he'll feel comfortable settling down with you.

Don't revel in being the damsel

Women often believe that men enjoy coming to their rescue, that it makes them feel masculine and needed, and yes, there is certainly truth to it to an extent. Many British chap don't get the chance to show their women how manly and strong they are much of the time, especially given how equal men and women are in so many ways these days. Therefore, give them an opportunity to let their masculinity shine, and they will often rise to the occasion. That's why you'll often find the British chap frequenting the good old DIY stores, aiming to fix things around the house. They'll often jump at the chance to get out their infamous toolbox (which may well be full of tools that were bought on a whim and are rarely used) to show you how well they can operate a drill or use a power saw. They may enjoy helping you put oil in your car or fix the dishwasher, as it gives them a chance to roll up their sleeves and prove to you they can take care of you.

The thing is, a lot of women love their chaps looking after them in this manner so much that they can often start to adopt a damsel in distress mentality, whereby they are constantly needing things from their partner. This may start innocently enough, with a few requests here and there, but sometimes it can develop so much that women become practically incapable of doing anything for themselves.

A client of mine, Rosie, was so happy to be moving in with her serious boyfriend Mike. They had found a new house together and were excited by the prospect of doing it up just the way they liked it. Mike was quite a dab hand at DIY, and so revelled in being on hand to sort out the refurbishment. He was the sort of chap who refused to hire in help as he knew everything from electrics to sanding floors, and Rosie was very proud of his knowledge and ability to get the job done. So much so that she started asking more and more of Mike. She'd start by asking him to fix the bathroom taps, which was fine. Then, when it came to moving day, she asked him to lift all the boxes of furniture and clothes, as everything was simply too heavy to lift herself. He graciously obliged. However, problems arose when Rosie started taking advantage of his kindness and Mike started to feel not like a chivalrous knight, but like a bit of a fool. Rosie would contact him at work and send him lists of jobs to be done, some of which she probably could have done herself, and then when he got home from a hard day at work she'd start requesting a foot rub and some dinner she liked.

It might come as no surprise, but Mike soon began to resent Rosie's demands, and what he deemed to be initially endearing, soon became needy and annoying. Whilst most guys will be happy to help you out once in a while, they are often much more willing to help you when they're not made to feel like they need to. If you act like you don't need their help that much, and like you're independent and could get on without him, they will be so much more willing to jump to attention and prove their manliness to you. That's not to say you should let them get away with doing nothing while you do it all yourself. The woman who tries to do it all will end up doing everything. Just be mindful how much you are asking of your chap. No man wants to feel like he's getting involved with anyone who's demanding too much of him.

Beware of talking for the sake of talking

I must confess, I too am often guilty of this one with my other half. Like many women, I enjoy discussing things just to talk. In fact, I'll often discuss issues of the day, or problems that may be on the horizon just to get them out there in the open. I don't necessarily want to find solutions to such topics of conversation. I simply want him to listen and empathise with what I'm talking about. However, many men find it incredibly hard to have a conversation without there seeming to be some sort of end goal or resolution.

For example, imagine the following typical conversation:

> Him: 'Hi darling, lovely to see you. How was your day?'
> Her: 'Oh it was alright, just terribly busy. I missed the train by two minutes so I had to wait thirty minutes on a freezing platform. It was so annoying.'

Now, what she would really like to hear from him at this stage is something along the lines of...

> Him: 'Oh you poor thing, you must be freezing. Let's run you a bath later. Why were you so busy?'

What she probably hears instead is something along the lines of...

> Him: 'Oh no well tomorrow make sure you leave earlier. Just make your excuses that you have a train to catch.'

You see, chaps are usually solution driven and will endeavour to help you by finding ways out of the perceived problem they are confronted with. Therefore, if their partner tells them they have an issue, then their immediate response is to try to resolve it. Rarely do they realise that we just want to talk for the sake of talking and because it makes us feel valued and appreciated if someone understands and listens. Very often, in fact, we'll get perturbed when our chaps will jump to a solution before we've felt we've been listened to. It's in instances like this when you hear women cry, 'Why don't you listen to me!' much to the bemusement of the man, of course, who thought he was being incredibly helpful by offering to find a way out of the perceived quandary.

When you're at this phase of your relationship, you're bound to be sharing your thoughts and feelings with each other, and conversations similar to the example before will no doubt start to sound familiar. If you want to chat but he's offering you solutions that you don't find particularly helpful, then just be mindful that it's not because he's trying to be annoying; it's just because he doesn't know any other way of dealing with the situation. If you do find yourself getting slightly annoyed by his perceived inability to empathise or understand, it doesn't hurt to point it out to him. I often jokingly turn to my other half and say, 'Darling, I'm quite happy to vent without looking for a solution!' and he often laughs because he simply doesn't realise he's doing it.

Don't ever stop singing his praises

The Brits are often terribly cautious with the amount of compliments they extend upon their partners. It's often quite ironic in fact given the amount of compliments women like to bestow upon other women. Yes, we've all been there, in the bathroom of a restaurant or at a party and you can't help but gush over how fabulous the other women look and how much you simply *love* their dress. Women, unlike men, often bond in Britain by complimenting each other and the more you are seen to be flattering, the more you are deemed likeable (however much you actually mean the compliment). Therefore, why is it that there appears to be some sort of compliment rationing going on when true relationships are formed. Now, I'm not saying we should all go around complimenting our significant other all the time insincerely; however, we should be as generous as we can be with dishing out compliments we truly mean. British men, especially, rarely hear compliments from their friends. It's simply not the done thing to be directly frank about one's feelings with chaps, so they'll often disguise it through 'banter' as we know. Therefore, they really do appreciate it when it comes from you.

It's not just because they like to hear the compliments to feel flattered. Yes, there is undoubtedly an element of that, as all men have an ego that they enjoy being stroked, but more importantly, complimenting him is crucial because it makes him feel you respect him, and respect is one of the most important veins running through any relationship. Make a note to compliment your man on something specific next time you see him. Don't just say, 'You look nice' but say, 'I love that shirt on you, it really suits you.' Also, don't forget to sing his praises in front of other people, too. Rave about him up in front of your friends, and remember to comment on how proud you are of him. He'll really appreciate it and you'll probably find he'll start complimenting you back more often too.

Boys will be boys

Boys will inevitably be boys for as long as women will allow them to be, and allow them we should, because giving your man the space he needs to enjoy his hobbies, interests and friends is incredibly healthy. Just because he might want to meet up with his old school friends for a few beers doesn't mean you have to incessantly message him asking him how it's going, or send him photos of yourself at home eating alone with a big sad face

– just let him be. In fact, whenever he's making plans with the boys, you should be aiming to do something really productive with your time too, so he sees you have other things going on other than him. It doesn't mean you have to arrange a rival girls night to compete with him and teach him a lesson for going out with his friends, but you can arrange to go to the gym, take up a new hobby, see friends you haven't seen for ages. A lot of the time people complain that when they get into relationships they stop doing things they perhaps loved doing before they met their partner, but it needn't be the case. Make time for yourself, and give your guy the space he needs to enjoy his time alone without you, too. Besides, absence does make the heart grow fonder, so you'll only have much more to catch up on when you do see each other.

Don't get too comfortable

Just because you're all settled into a nice relationship doesn't mean you have an excuse to not make an effort anymore with regards looking after yourself. Unfortunately, this does work both ways and men can be just as guilty as women in this respect, but if you find your relationship suddenly starts to revolve more around movie nights and takeaways rather than activities, watch out; you might be getting a little too comfortable. Even if your partner is keen to relax and be lazy every now and then, he may well have a higher metabolism than you, so be sure you continue to look after yourself. In fact, when you have a lovely partner, you have to work just as hard if not harder to maintain the relationship as it was right at the beginning.

Don't mention the whole marriage thing, though

Much like the notion of bringing up the three little words, 'I love you', when dealing with a British man, you're really best placed not mentioning the fact that you're keen to get married, if indeed you are. Many British chaps respond to a woman not wanting to get married much more positively than those who are seemingly pressuring them into it. In fact, sometimes women who are resolutely keen to not get married can, without realising it, subject their chaps to reverse psychology and make them inherently keener on the idea.

One of my clients, Geoffrey, was this way inclined. When I met him, he openly told me that he really wasn't looking for marriage at the moment, and although I respected his honesty, I had a feeling he just hadn't met the right girl yet. I introduced Geoffrey to a fabulous French friend of mine who was a breath of fresh air to the usual type of girls he went for. She had her own life, her own independence and she owned her own mind, so she most certainly did not want to get married for a while. This shocked Geoffrey so much that he couldn't help but find her the most fascinating creature he had ever laid eyes on, and he went full steam ahead into pursuing her. She was unmoved by his advances, and although she thought he was charming enough, it took a lot of work from Geoffrey's part to convince her he was a worthy catch. Eventually the two of them got together, but still to this day Geoffrey continually suggests marriage to his lovely French lady, and she continuously rejects him.

Funnily enough, and just to give you all a bit more context to this story, this was the same girl who, after they had been dating for two years, also refused to move in with Geoffrey. He kept asking and asking and she would continuously say she wasn't ready. One day, he got so fed up with her rebuffs that he just went out and bought a flat for them both and surprised her when he signed the contract, picked up the keys and welcomed her to her new home. She didn't exactly say no when that happened, as you can imagine.

OK, so this may not be your typical scenario and it doesn't happen to every girl, but truth be told there is some wisdom to be learnt from her lack of interest in marriage and commitment. It only made her partner more interested in the notion of settling down.

Don't drop hints about the 'M' word until he does, don't go to friends' weddings and subtly mention what you would and wouldn't like at your wedding, don't complain how many weddings you have to attend this year, just be rather indifferent about the whole 'M' thing until he brings it up himself. As we have learned, men like to feel like they have something to conquer, so let him feel he has to fight to win you over, rather than making it all too obvious he's done that already.

The Very British Rules When Things Go Wrong

As much as I have revelled in the journey of imagining all your dating successes up until this point, wistfully envisioning you all finding and keeping your ultimate, eligible knight, I am, after all, a realist and must confess that there are certain times when relationships simply don't go to plan. For whatever reason, certain rocks are laid across our relationship road, endeavouring to trip us up or catch us off guard. This is especially the case when dealing with a British chap, as they rarely know how to express themselves, so there are invariably times when we can be left scratching our heads wondering what on earth went wrong.

For this reason, I wanted to set aside a chapter specifically dedicated to the very British rules of dating should things not quite go in the streamlined manner, which I have been aspiring to describe until now. Whilst we are inevitably eloquent and charming ladies, we are after all human, so certain things will invariably not always go quite to plan.

Accidents happen...

You've had a one night stand

If you have gone on a glorious 'date' with a chap and found yourself succumbing to his advances and offers of a 'nightcap' – which, as we all know, inexorably leads to one thing – then you might have to re-evaluate your stance on the relationship. Unfortunately, very rarely do chaps consider you the same once they have won you over, and your value will immediately be deemed lower to them had you held out (for lack of a better word) that little bit longer. However, accidents do happen, so ask yourself whether you genuinely like this man. Is he really *Mr Right* or is he probably more *Mr Right Now*?

If he's the latter, and that's what you want, then that's fine so long as expectations continue to be managed and you don't start falling in love with him, and hope that he'll grow to realise how amazing you are and decide he wants to have a relationship with you. These kids of men are driven to get you into bed, not to fall in love, so don't start thinking you can change him.

If you do genuinely like him and this happens, then all is not necessarily lost. The best thing you can do is make sure you are as unforgettable to him as possible, and leave a lasting impression. So don't just rest on your laurels with the fact that you are an attractive lady, but you need to ensure you're unmistakeably funny, charming and independent too, so he continues to be attracted to you. Give him something more to work towards other than sleeping with you, so don't make yourself too readily available, and only give him titbits of information about yourself, so he will want to get to know more. It also doesn't hurt to leave a good impression in the bedroom department, so make sure you don't overlook how important men consider sexual chemistry to be. Often, attractive ladies tend to rely too heavily on their appearance, but truth be told, this can generally only get you so far. Your looks may get your into his bedroom, but it takes a lot more than that to keep you there.

Also, don't beat yourself up too much if you have made a mistake. Sometimes if you walk away with your head held high and your confidence beaming, his interest will continue to be piqued and intrigued by you. You should probably also ask yourself whether you really want to have a relationship with someone with such a lifestyle. Perhaps, unlike you, he does this all the time.

If you've stayed the night after a dalliance, just make sure you're not outstaying your welcome. Don't hang around too long making chit-chat and having small talk the next morning. British men are often at a loss for things to say when approaching you, let alone the morning after sleeping with you. If you really don't feel all that awkward about it all, I am willing to bet that he will, so do yourself a favour and make your excuses to leave. Even if he offers breakfast, it's probably because he's just trying to be polite. Besides, you're a busy lady, you've got a lot going on in your life and he's had enough of your precious time already.

You stayed the night

If you accidentally fell asleep at his house before you were ready to have sex with him, then be mindful not to do this again until you are. British chaps think that when you are willing to stay over, you are willing to have sex with them, so be careful not to give them this impression until you feel the relationship is at a point at which you're comfortable with doing it. So if he suggests that you should go to his house and watch a film, he's blatantly trying to sleep with you. In this case, don't give him too much satisfaction by staying the night too – even if nothing happens. Just be elusive and unobtainable for as long as you can and go home. In an ideal situation you shouldn't really be going to his house for the first few dates anyway, as it's crucial during this phase that he puts in the effort to romance you. If he's hoping to get the goods without doing the work, I'm afraid he's probably only after one thing and certainly isn't worthy of your time.

If you had a dalliance with a work colleague

Should something happen between you and a work colleague this can be very tricky ground. The Brits do not like to face up to the aftermath of such instances and would often rather avoid or ignore one another entirely rather than talk about or face up to what happened, even if there is notable chemistry. The humiliation that comes with the barrage of gossip from all corners of the office is enough to put both parties off actually mentioning it again.

The best thing to do in such a situation, should an accident happen at a work Christmas party after one too many 'Merry Sherrys', is to work out whether it was a cringe-worthy mistake that you really regret, or actually something that made you smile from ear to ear when it happened. If it's something that you didn't intend to happen and you'd rather forget that it did, then the best thing to do is to just be polite and gracious about the whole thing. If there are too many prying eyes at the office, send the chap an email or a message via instant messenger making light of the situation. Let him know you're not fazed whatsoever and the ice will inevitably start to break.

If you've had a dalliance with someone that you genuinely like and have rather fancied for a while, then just take it slowly and see how it goes. Be sure to keep things under wraps from your colleagues for as long as you can, or at least until you both equally feel comfortable that there is a story to be told. Should anyone pry you for gossip prematurely you can simply smile and say 'Don't you know a lady never tells.' There's no need to add fuel to flame that may fizzle anyway, and besides it's nobody else's business but your own.

Why is he being weird?

Why hasn't he called or texted?

Most of us have been there. You've met a great guy and have exchanged numbers only to never hear from him again. Or you may have been out a couple of times only for him to disappear into the oblivion without saying a word. Yes, men are rather complex creatures and it's often terribly hard to work out what is going through their minds in order to understand why on earth someone who initially seemed so keen has suddenly vanished.

There are a whole host of reasons why he might not call you back, and each circumstance is very unique, but more often than not the British man says a huge amount more by what he doesn't do than what he does. Therefore, despite how lovely your dates might have been with him, you have to listen very carefully to what he's not saying or doing to pick up on what he's really feeling, as it's very unlikely he will articulate himself clearly through the spoken word.

Truth is that if you have had a great date but he doesn't call you, it's because he doesn't want to. If you meet a great guy but he never gets in touch despite you getting on famously, it's because he doesn't want to. British men very often try to be as charming and polite to your face as they can be, as they all want to be seen to be the nice guy, when in reality they are thinking other things entirely. I can't reiterate it enough: if a guy genuinely wanted to follow up he would find a way to call you. Don't let yourself think that he's too busy, that he may have lost your number or that he's travelling a lot for work. If a chap is really interested he will find the time. A man who doesn't follow through doesn't want to move things along, and so rather than say so himself, he's letting his silence speak for itself.

The same can be said for when a guy inconsistently texts or calls you. Let's say you go on a great date, then don't hear from him for a few days before he messages you. You text him back and then he takes another few days to reply. This guy is not serious about you or progressing things, as if he were he'd be ensuring his contact was more considered. A chap who is interested is keen to make a good impression, and so he will be mindful not to leave it too long before messaging or calling you. If he doesn't really care that much then, he's simply not showing you the respect you deserve, and I'm afraid to say, he's just not that interested.

As much as it can be frustrating if you don't hear from him, it's important to let him lead in terms of contacting you. If you've gone out for a date, absolutely never be the one to follow up afterwards, let him do it. If he doesn't, then I'm afraid to say, and to quote the ever famous book/film, 'He's just not that into you,' and you're much better off waiting it out for someone who is.

Why has he stopped texting?

If you've been seeing a guy for a while, perhaps you've been on a few dates, and he's been getting in touch consistently, then it can be quite exciting as it can outwardly seem like it's all going really well. You start to look forward to that daily text or phone call all the while thinking of witty responses to keep the flow of conversation going. You might appear to get on really well and have fantastic chemistry, when all of a sudden the text messages start to slow down or worse still, stop altogether. Your daily contact might start to decrease to every other day, and each time he appears to be taking longer and longer to respond. If this is the case, beware, as it's likely the chap is starting to cool. A woman's intuition is a strong thing when these things happen, so have a think about why this may be the case. Perhaps you've hit a point in your relationship when it's got to go from 'dating' to being a couple, and the chap has started to question whether that's really what he wants. If you're seeing a guy who isn't sure he wants to be in a relationship, it usually won't last longer than around the 90 day mark. During this time, he may be super keen to woo you, and wine and dine you, but when push comes to shove and it's decision time as to whether or not to take things further, he'll be out of there to move onto the next shiny thing that catches his eye. A decrease in contact at around the 2-3 month phase is therefore something to be wary of. If you suspect his interest is waning, then make sure you're keeping yourself as busy as you can and that you don't give off any indications that you're keen to settle down into a relationship. Whatever you do, don't panic that you're losing him and try to 'persuade' him to regain his lost interest. It will only make things worse. Just detach yourself from him for a while if you can until he's ready to treat you how you deserve to be treated.

Why did he end it?

I got a phone call from one of my clients recently, who was absolutely devastated as she had been going out with a guy she really liked for two months when all of a sudden he just sent her a text message out of the blue to say the chemistry just wasn't there and that there was no point taking things further. By TEXT! Once I got past the initial shock of how disgraceful his behaviour was to not even be man enough to call her, or better still, arrange to meet in person, I was genuinely as surprised as she was that this had happened. From what I had gathered each date had been amazing, magical, and full of banter and laughter. They got on really well, they were messaging practically daily and starting to become more ingrained in each other's lives – so what went wrong all of a sudden and how come he just changed his tune seemingly overnight?

The first ninety days of any relationship can be the most testing, as it's often around this time that a relationship will either become established or unfortunately have to come to an end. As much as the dates during this phase can often seem to be going so ostensibly well, if a guy isn't keen on having a serious relationship, it doesn't matter what you do or how gorgeous you are, as there's no deviating a man from his desire for freedom. My client is genuinely stunning with lots to say for herself, but it frankly wouldn't matter how gorgeous the girl is if the chap isn't ready, as there's not much that can be done to change that.

Think about it this way, if a guy *were* interested in having a serious, committed relationship and you get on well and have wonderful dates, it's very likely he would continue to want to see you just to see how it goes, as there's no immediate need to end things. If however, he doesn't want to settle down or he doesn't see it going anywhere, he will be able to end it there and then. Men have a funny way of being able to compartmentalise their emotions. For example, they can break up with someone, then go straight back to work like nothing happened. We, as women, are very different, as when we feel something for someone it tends to be an all-encompassing emotion, and we simply can't box our feelings into separate categories. It's for this very reason that we find it all the more baffling when a chap is able to break things off so resolutely.

Therefore, my client was truly and unceremoniously dumped by text and was, quite justifiably, left in a true state of shock. If this happens to you, don't start wondering what it is you did wrong or how you could have changed the course of fate. There is often nothing you could do, as if a guy just isn't ready, he isn't ready. It's very much about timing and finding a guy at the right time of his life for a serious relationship, and ironically it can often not be with the girl he's not fundamentally best suited to. One of my male clients once told me, when he was about to get married, that there was in fact a girl who he was probably more compatible with and whom he went out with five years prior to meeting his soon-to-be wife, but he just wasn't ready at that time to settle down. It doesn't matter how amazing you are, don't think you can be the one to make him want to get married. If he isn't there yet, there's not much you can do other than find someone else who is.

Go Forth

Well my lovelies, it's time to go forth into the British dating world. I know it can be tricky, but hopefully you're now armed with a bit more understanding into the British gent's psyche than you were before. Just remember, quality men do exist and they are everywhere, they just need a little more gentle encouragement than other nations to come out of their romantically inept shells. Encourage them, be confident, be articulate, be fabulous and your charm will soon be so infectious you will be fighting them off! Please do let me know how you get on with your dating adventures, I'd love to hear from you so feel free to follow me on Twitter @LadyLaraAsprey and keep me up to date with any upcoming dates or to ask me any questions. I'll do my best to get back to as many of you as I can.

Good luck you eligible lot!

All the best,

Lara xxx

Dates for Your Diary

March

The Cheltenham Festival

What is it? Often considered the start of the Season, it's a four day annual flat horse racing event
Where is it? Cheltenham, Gloucestershire.
When? Mid March from Tuesday to Friday (Ladies Day is Wednesday).
Is there a dress code? No, as the races are mostly held in the winter they do not require a dress code. Many Ladies, however, do wear hats in the Club's enclosure.
How to buy tickets: Tickets can be bought from the beginning of September either online or by phone.
Fun facts: The prize money is second only to the Grand National held a few weeks later, with each race commanding around £500,000.
Tips: You can get a local or charter helicopter flight to the Festival should you wish to truly arrive in style!

Oxford Literary Festival

What is it? An annual festival consisting of events and speakers from all walks of literary life discussing a wide range of topics.

Where is it? Several venues in Oxford.

When? The end of March for one week.

Is there a dress code? No, you are very much free to wear what you like. Attendees are likely to be conservative, though, so you're no doubt better off dressing elegantly.

How to buy tickets: You can buy tickets online or by phone several months prior to the Festival.

Fun facts: Often some of the world's most respected authors attend including Seamus Heaney, Hilary Mantel and Julian Barnes.

Tips: Apart from the Festival itself you can also join lunches and dinners with some of the great literary writers. Check the Festival Programme for more details. You might find yourself sitting next to someone with whom you share keen interests.

April

The Boat Race

What is it? The Oxford vs. Cambridge boat race held annually in London.

Where is it? From Putney to Mortlake the race is four and a quarter mile long.

When? Early April.

Is there a dress code? No dress code. It's usually a pretty casual occasion.

How to buy tickets: You don't need to buy tickets, crowds just gather along the Thames to watch it and nearby pubs and bars are full of opportunities to mingle.

Fun facts: 2015 was the first year that the Women's Boat race will take place on the same day as the men, having previously taken place in Henley.

Tips: Pubs will be busy so if you're planning on watching from one, head down early to ensure you get a good view.

May

The Chelsea Flower Show

What is it? The Royal Horticultural Society's annual garden show.

Where is it? Chelsea, London.

When? Towards the end of May each year, for one week.

Is there a dress code? No, unless you attend on the Monda,y which is the only formal day, there is no official dress code. Practical dress is advised, however.

How to buy tickets: General tickets sell out fast each year so book early via their website.

Fun facts: Apparently it attracts more FTSE 100 chief executives than any other social event.

Tips: The first two days are traditionally for RHS members only. However, for a small fee, anyone can become a member.

BMW PGA Golf Championship

What is it? One of the most prestigious events in the golfing calendar and the flagship event of the European Tour.

Where is it? Wentworth, Surrey.

When? Around the third week of May each year for four days.

Is there a dress code? There is no specific dress code for attendance to the PGA's 'tented village', but should you wish to enter the Clubhouse you will need to follow their strict rules, so it's best to check their website for more information. Also be mindful to bring comfortable shoes if you plan to walk around the golf course.

How to buy tickets: Tickets can be bought via the PGA website.

Fun facts: In 2014 around 100,000 spectators attended the PGA including celebrities such as David Ginola, Jamie Redknapp, Bed Foden and Sir Steve Redgrave.

Tips: Be mindful that mobile phones aren't permitted on any of the courses or in the communal rooms of the Wentworth Club.

The Glyndebourne Festival

What is it? One of the finest opera houses in a beautiful and picturesque setting.

Where is it? Lewes, East Sussex.

When? From late May until late August each year.

Is there a dress code? Despite it being a daytime event, evening dress is customary (although not essential) so you'll see most people enjoying their picnics in black tie.

How to buy tickets: Tickets are very sought after and, although they become available to the public in late March, they do sell out very quickly. Alternatively, you can pay an annual fee to become an Associate Member, after which you will probably have to wait ten years before being able to become a full Member.

Fun facts: The auditorium, which opened in 1994, now seats 1,200 people.

Tips: Although you can bring your own picnic you can also hire the Glyndebourne traditional picnic, which comes complete with a three course meal, champagne, porter service, and furniture.

June

Royal Academy Summer Exhibition

What is it? The world's largest open-submission art exhibition.

Where is it? The Royal Academy, Piccadilly, London.

When? From June to mid August.

Is there a dress code? If you attend the Preview Party in June, the dress code is 'Glamorous', otherwise you are free to dress as you please.

How to buy tickets: Ticket to the Preview Party can be bought via their website if booked early enough. To visit all the exhibitions for free you can become a Friend of the Academy from £97 per year.

Fun facts: Caroline Taggart in her book 'Her Ladyship's Guide to the British Season' described the husband potential of this event as 'Dazzling, there is absolutely no knowing who you might meet'.

Tips: It does help to have at least some interest in art as there are upwards of 1,400 pieces of art to admire.

Queen's Club Championship

What is it? An annual tournament for male tennis players held on grass.

Where is it? The Queen's Club, West Kensington.

When? For one week in mid June.

Is there a dress code? Smart casual is generally fine as there is no specific dress code.

How to buy tickets: You can buy tickets via their website from early March to access either Centre Court, Court one or ground admission.

Fun facts: It is often regarded as a warm up to Wimbledon, and draws impressive crowds each year.

Tips: If you can get access to the Roof Garden for a couple of glasses of champagne, it's truly worth it!

The Derby

What is it? A prominent fixture on the horseracing calendar.

Where is it? Epsom Downs, Surrey.

When? Held over two days on the first weekend of June.

Is there a dress code? Official dress codes apply only in the Queen's Stand and are more stringent on Derby Day (Sat) than Ladies Day (Fri). For general admission all guests are encouraged to dress up, with ladies wearing a hat/fascinator and gentlemen a jacket, collar and tie.

How to buy tickets: Like most events of the Season, it's advisable to book early. Check their website for more information.

Fun facts: During the two World Wars many events of the Season were suspended. The Derby, however, simply moved from Epsom to Newmarket.

Tips: Try to arrive as early as you can as the crowds descending upon the Derby over the two days can be significant.

Royal Ascot

What is it? The most famous horseracing event of the year.

Where is it? Ascot, Berkshire.

When? From Tuesday to Saturday in the third week of June.

Is there a dress code? There are fairly strict dress code rules for those guests who enter the Royal Enclosure and slightly less restrictive rules for those who enter the Grandstand.

However, standards for the dress code have famously been slipping.

How to buy tickets: You must be sponsored by a guest who has attended on four previous occasions in order to get into the Royal Enclosure, but anyone can get tickets to the Grandstand.

Fun facts: The Queen has attended every year, each year joining for a full four days. Each day begins with a Royal Procession where the Royal Family and their guests arrive in (weather permitting) open carriages.

Tips: In 2012 the organisers of Royal Ascot made revisions to the dress code to the Royal Enclosure as people were failing to dress in what was deemed to be an acceptable manner. Don't try to get away with an outfit that's verging on the unacceptable.

The Championships (Wimbledon)

What is it? Regarded as the most prestigious tennis tournament in the world.

Where is it? Wimbledon, London.

When? It takes place over two weeks from late June - early July.

Is there a dress code? The players are the ones subject to the most stringent dress codes while spectators are encouraged to be smart-casual.

How to buy tickets: You'll need to submit an application form to the All England's Tennis Club by mid December to get entered into the ballot. From there, you can simply hope you'll be lucky enough to get selected. Either that or you can choose to join the famous queues.

Fun facts: Players used to bow or curtsy to the members of the Royal Family seated in the Royal box when they entered or left Centre Court. In 2003, however, the Duke of Kent decided this was only required should the Queen or Prince of Wales be present.

Tips: The best time to go is the first week if you can as there are the most matches. Make sure you take an umbrella!

Chestertons Polo in the Park

What is it? The nearest polo event to central London.

Where is it? Hurlingham Park, Fulham.

When? Usually the first week of June over a long weekend

Is there a dress code? Although no formal dress code is required, it is advised to dress elegantly. Summer dresses are fine but if you choose to wear heels you're better off with wedges or using heel protectors if you can (often you can buy these there).

How to buy tickets: You can buy grandstand tickets via their website. They book out fast though, so make sure you buy them in advance.

Fun facts: The polo field is smaller than usual, meaning you'll be very close to the action on the day.

Tips: Saturday is Ladies Day and by far the day with the most atmosphere. Head to the Mahiki bar or the Champagne Lanson Garden for great people watching.

The Prince of Wales Trophy Cup

What is it? The traditional opener to some of the bigger polo tournaments.

Where is it? The Royal Berkshire Polo Club located just outside Windsor.

When? The second week of June (it used to take place late May).

Is there a dress code? Same as 'Mint Polo in the Park'.

How to buy tickets: Same as 'Mint Polo in the Park'.

Fun facts: In 2015 the Royal County of Berkshire Polo Club celebrated their 30th anniversary.

Tips: There are a whole host of new events and plans from 2015 onwards, so check the website for the latest developments.

Glorious Goodwood

What is it? The Festival of Speed is an annual motoring motor show.

Where is it? The Goodwood Estate, Chichester.

When? The third week of June each year over a three day weekend.

Is there a dress code? No, the event is pretty casual and as the event is outdoors they usually advise you to wear comfortable shoes and prepare for the unpredictable British weather.

How to buy tickets: Tickets are usually available from November the year before and can be purchased via their website.

Fun facts: The Goodwood Estate is run by Lord March, who took over from his father, the 10th Duke of Richmond, after his death in 1994. His grandfather was also a car aficionado and converted a wartime aerodrome into a motor racing circuit in 1948.

Tips: The style at Goodwood is casual but effortlessly chic, so make an understated effort if you go. It's certainly always plentiful with charming chaps so is well worth a visit.

Henley Regatta

What is it? The most famous regatta in the World.

Where is it? Henley, Berkshire.

When? Late June - early July over five day (Wed - Sun).

Is there a dress code? Yes, there are strict dress codes to those attending the Stewards' Enclosure. Even though there is no official dress code for the Regatta Enclosure most people choose to dress formally anyway.

How to buy tickets: You can buy tickets to the Regatta's Enclosure online, but access to the Stewards' Enclosure is only given to members and their guests.

Fun facts: They are vigilant about the use of mobile phones. Anyone caught repeatedly making or receiving calls in the Stewards' Enclosure will be escorted out and will have their badge forfeited.

Tips: Don't bring a picnic or your own food and drink. You won't be allowed in with it.

July

Henley Festival

What is it? A Festival of music, theatre, comedy, literature and art.
Where is it? Henley, Berkshire.
When? Early July over five evenings.
Is there a dress code? Black tie for gentlemen and long or short evening wear for ladies.
How to buy tickets: You can book tickets via their website or for more booking options you can become a member.
Fun facts: The Festival began in 1983 and each year draws some amazing artists from the world of stage and sound.
Tips: The crowd is generally a bit older and wiser at the Festival than the Regatta, and so it tends to be somewhat more refined.

International Polo

What is it? A highlight of the polo season. Previously sponsored by Cartier and then Audi.
Where is it? Guards Polo Club, near Windsor in Berkshire.
When? Usually at the end of July.
Is there a dress code? Although no formal dress code is required it is advised to dress elegantly. Summer dresses

are fine but if you choose to wear heels you're better off with wedges or using heel protectors if you can (often you can buy these at the events themselves).

How to buy tickets: You can book tickets via their website or get hospitality packages on The Smiths Lawn.

Fun facts: It was known as the Cartier polo for many years, but rumour has they ceased being associated with it due to the fact it became regarded as less and less prestigious.

Tips: Even if you don't get tickets it's fun to organise a picnic in your car, and drive up and park. There's usually lots of atmosphere.

Cowdray Park

What is it? Also known as Gold Cup or 'British Open' it's the pinnacle of the polo season.

Where is it? Midhurst, West Sussex.

When? The third week of July each year.

Is there a dress code? Same as 'International Polo'.

How to buy tickets: You can book tickets via their website.

Fun facts: It used to be known as the Veuve Cliquot Gold Cup until 2015 when Jaeger-Le Coultre was confirmed as the new title sponsor.

Tips: It doesn't hurt to know a bit about the sport. A chukka is seven and a half minutes long, and there are four to eight in each game. Teams swap ends after each goal.

August

Cowes Week

What is it? A spectacular sailing regatta.
Where is it? The Isle of Wight.
When? One week in early August.
Is there a dress code? No it's generally pretty casual, unless you are invited to a ball or parties on board a boat, in which case there can be terribly formal dress codes.
How to buy tickets: You don't need a ticket unless you wish to attend a yacht club ball, but to do that you will need to know a member.
Fun facts: During Cowes Week there are up to 40 races a day and around 100,000 spectators.
Tips: Friday is the best day to go as there are fantastic fireworks on the water in the Cowes Harbour.

End Notes

_____

1. The Future of Dating Summary Report, eHarmony, Third City and The Future Foundation 2013
2. Personality: Evolutionary Heritage and Human Distinctiveness, Arnold H. Buss
3. Watching the English, 2004, Kate Fox
4. Texting Statistics http://consumers.ofcom.org.uk/news/the-text-message-turns-20-today
5. WhattsApp vs Texting, https://medium.com/@DaleJGraham/whatsapp-vs-texting-2015-statistics-8f3de11d0824
6. Personality Temperaments Theory. http://www.interstrength.com/content/temperament_theory

Acknowledgements

So many wonderful people have helped me in the writing of this book. Many thanks to my mother for her constant support and encouragement, my friends and clients for their honesty and openness in discussing their love lives with me and everybody I have tirelessly asked for help with my research.

Thank you to Thomas Murphy PR for your infectious determination and sense of urgency and Stephanie Reed at So Vain Books for believing in this book and making it a reality. Your attention to detail has been amazing and it's been a real pleasure to share the journey with you both.

A special thanks for my wonderful partner and friend JC, for being so patient, supportive and understanding and for letting me believe anything is possible.

And, of course, not forgetting all the wonderful men and women out there who have helped and inspired me to write this and have no idea I've written about them. I've enjoyed listening attentively to your stories so long may that continue!

Index